Passenger Routes

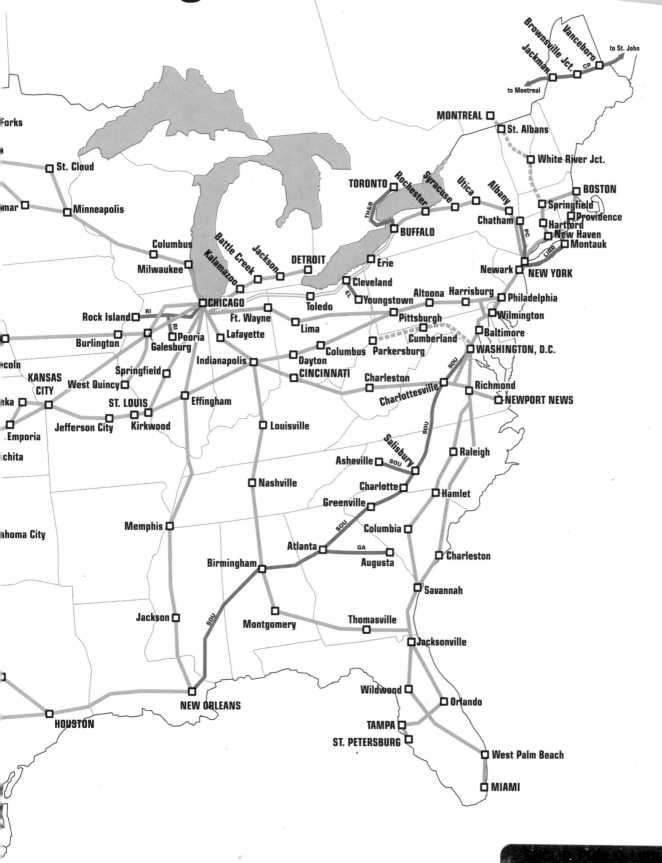

AMTRAK

BRIAN SOLOMON

MBI

Dedication

To Doug Riddell—Amtrak locomotive engineer, gifted journalist,
and a very good friend.

First published in 2004 by MBI, an imprint of MBI Publishing Company, Galtier Plaza, Suite 200, 380 Jackson Street, St. Paul, MN 55101-3885 USA

The information in this book is true and complete to the best of our knowledge. All recommendations are made without any guarantee on the part of the author or Publisher, who also disclaim any liability incurred in connection with the use of this data or specific details.

This publication has not been prepared, approved, or licensed by Amtrak. We recognize, further, that some words, model names, and designations mentioned herein are the property of the trademark holder. We use them for identification purposes only. This is not an official publication.

MBI titles are also available at discounts in bulk quantity for industrial or sales-promotional use. For details write to Special Sales Manager at Motorbooks International Wholesalers & Distributors, Galtier Plaza, Suite 200, 380 Jackson Street, St. Paul, MN 55101-3885 USA.

ISBN 0-7603-1765-8

Printed in China

Front endpapers: Amtrak passenger routes, 1972. *Otto Vondrak illustration*

Back endpapers: Amtrak passenger routes, 2004. *Otto Vondrak illustration*

On the frontispiece: The state of California funded a portion of Amtrak's 1988 order for Horizon Cars, so some were assigned to California services, such as the Oakland-Bakersfield *San Joaquins* and later the San Jose-Sacramento *Capitols*. In August 1992, train No. 722, the morning Capitol Corridor service (San Jose-Sacramento) at Oakland's 16th Street Station consists of three-year-old Horizon Cars. Today, California Cars are standard equipment on the Capitol Corridor trains. *Brian Solomon*

On the title page: Train No. 8, the eastward *Empire Builder*, approaches Browning, Montana, on the Burlington Northern on July 8, 1994. *Brian Solomon*

On the back cover: Amtrak F40PH 358 and four Horizon Cars make up Capitol Corridor No. 726. The train catches the evening glint as it skirts the shore of San Pablo Bay at Pinole, California, on its way from San Jose to Sacramento in the summer of 1992. *Brian Solomon*

Edited by Dennis Pernu
Designed by Chris Fayers

CONTENTS

ACKNOWLEDGMENTS

The generosity and enthusiasm of Amtrak supporters must never be underestimated. A great many people helped in the preparation of this book. Thanks to Tim Doherty for his loan of books and materials, plus intellectual discussion of passenger transport and planning. Pat Yough gave me use of his library, loaned photographs, and arranged for interviews, plus helped in proofreading and map adjustment. Thanks to Otto M. Vondrak for map work. Robert A. Buck helped in many ways, proofreading texts, offering suggestions, and making innumerable introductions to key people involved with the Amtrak story. Thanks to David Clinton for loaning books and articles, and for his enthusiasm. Brian Jennison opened many doors and helped with proofreading, captioning, and syntax. Fred Matthews offered perspective on passenger operations and loaned me books, photographs, and other literature.

Between 1994 and 1996, I worked at Pentrex Publishing in Waukesha, Wisconsin, as an associate editor of *Passenger Train Journal* (*PTJ*), which provided my introduction to many people in the industry, including Doug Riddell, who became one of that publication's columnists. In the production of this book, Doug has given me his support, made introductions, provided photographs, and he and his wife, Sandy, hosted me on visits to Richmond, Virginia. John Gruber has been very supportive and provided the sidebar on Gil Reid. Clark Johnson Jr. helped put Amtrak, its equipment, and its personalities in better perspective. Craig Willett provided wit and helpful contacts.

Special thanks to everyone in North Carolina involved in passenger operations, planning, and railroad maintenance. Especially kind were Amtrak's Jim McDaniel and Jeff Mann, the North Carolina Department of Transportation's Julia Hegele, and North Carolina Railroad's Keri Towery. Thanks to J. J. Grumblatt Jr. for helping with data on passenger cars, Turboliners, and Metroliners.

My father Richard Jay Solomon brought me on my first train ride, handed me my first camera, and collected thousands of railway documents. In addition, he provided personal recollections of Senator Claiborne Pell, Alan Boyd, John Volpe, and other key figures involved in Amtrak's early years. He also helped proofread my text and contributed photographs. Thanks also to Walter Zullig, Paul Reistrup, Claire Nolan, Thomas M. Hoover, George W. Kowanski, Ciara Dawson, Bruce Heard, and Vic Stone.

The making of railway photographs involves a complex process of decision-making, light, equipment manipulation, film choice, and luck. Many people have aided me in my travels to study and photograph railway operations. In addition to many of the people already thanked, my quest in railway image-making was aided by several fellow photographers: Mel Patrick, T. S. Hoover, Michael L. Gardner, Tom and Mike Danneman, J. D. Schmid, Bob Krambles, Blair Kooistra, Scott Bontz, Mike Abalos, Norm Yellin, John Peters, Doug Eisele, David Monte Verde, Will Holloway, Vic Neves, Don Marson, George and Candy Pitarys, Joe Quinlan, Gerald Hook, Brandon Delany, Mark Hemphill, Pete Reusch, Jon Roma, Brian Plant, Doug Moore, Brian Rutherford, Dean Sauvola, Joe McMillan, Sean-Graham White, Dick Gruber, Marshall Beecher, George C. Corey, Tim Hensch, and Mark Leppert. In addition to my own photographs, I reviewed thousands of images for consideration in this book. Contributing photographers are credited appropriately by their images. Thanks to Michael L. Gardner, who gave me the use of his darkroom to make black-and-white prints.

In addition to personal observation, exploration, and interviews, I read hundreds of documents, books, magazine articles, newspapers, railroad literature, operating manuals, guidebooks, reports, and government publications in preparing this book. Among the most useful were articles by Don Phillips in *TRAINS* magazine and the *Washington Post*; David P. Morgan's monthly editorials in *TRAINS*; contemporary articles in *TRAINS* by Bob Johnston; Frank Wilner's excellent 1994 book *The Amtrak Story*, which helped me comprehend the railway's historical financial struggles; and *PTJ*, which under the stewardship of Mike Schafer, and later Carl Swanson, helped keep the spirit of American passenger railroading alive in a world dominated by highway transport.

Thanks to my brother Seán Solomon and mother Maureen Solomon for support and trips on Amtrak. I've made every effort to ensure accuracy. If errors appear, they are my own, and not those of the many people who gave their expertise.

At sunset on September 30, 1991, Amtrak No. 449, the westward Boston section of the *Lake Shore Limited,* meets eastward Conrail freight SERE (Selkirk, New York, to Readville, Massachusetts) on the former Boston & Albany east of Palmer, Massachusetts. Amtrak trains must share track space with freight traffic. *Brian Solomon*

I come from a family of train-riders. From the 1920s to after World War II, my grandfather, Alfred Solomon, traveled the country by Pullman sleeper selling nurses uniforms. He preferred to travel on lines with good dining car service. "The B&O always had the best food," he told me. My father, Richard Jay Solomon, is an ardent railway traveler and a regular Amtrak rider. He has traveled hundreds of thousands of miles on American rails and on railways around the world. Between my father and I, we have ridden virtually every Amtrak service. He takes the train every couple of weeks, usually up and down the Northeast Corridor (NEC), and occasionally westward from New England or along the Pacific Coast. I ride Amtrak as often as I can, and I've traveled by train in more than 20 countries. One of my favorite trips is the *Lake Shore Limited* to Chicago.

Amtrak is a difficult subject to write about. It is difficult to mention Amtrak to anyone without receiving an impassioned response. Its employees, riders, historians, critics, and foes each have deep-seated opinions. Making my job especially challenging was trying to sum up everything that culminated with Amtrak's creation while telling its 33-year history in just 25,000 words and 150 illustrations.

Amtrak has a complex personality. I think of Amtrak as the scrawny stepson of aged, jaded, and once-wealthy parents who must make his way through the streets in an out-of-style and awkwardly fitting suit. Yet, despite constant ridicule from bullies, he keeps his chin up and smiles. When he has to, he stands and fights for his right

At 7:19 a.m. on the winter solstice in 1992, Amtrak No. 88, the *Silver Meteor*, rolls across the Susquehanna River at Havre de Grace, Maryland. *Brian Solomon*

to live. He has the will to survive and, more importantly, friends to help him. He's just been waiting for someone to give him the resources to do the job he was born to do. Then, Amtrak will be a hero.

Amtrak was created because although the American people wanted passenger trains as a transport option, American freight railroads could no longer afford to subsidize the operation of passenger services from freight profits. Amtrak was hastily planned and poorly financed from the very beginning and it has struggled ever since because, unlike all other transport modes, it does not have a secure source of funding. In fact, Amtrak presents a funding anomaly. With most American transport, government funding supports basic infrastructure while private industry

provides services. Under Amtrak's legislated structure, local, state, and federal governments make up the deficit between the costs of service and fare-box revenue, while most of the infrastructure outside of the NEC is privately owned and managed. Amtrak has to pay for the use of the tracks, in effect making Amtrak a customer of railroads.

Long-distance passenger trains are a valuable resource. When all costs are weighed, trains provide one of the most economical transport solutions. Furthermore, passengers are afforded a more comfortable, less stressful journey than is possible with automobiles, buses, or airplanes. Riding a train has long been considered one of the best ways to experience America. Trains are also one of the safest means of ground transport and are vastly safer than automobiles. In an age when more than 40,000 people die annually in automobile accidents, this is an important consideration. You are also far more likely to be struck by lightning than killed as an Amtrak passenger. The National Weather Service estimates that during a 30-year period there are an average of 69 annual fatalities from lightning strikes. The yearly average of all Amtrak *and* commuter rail passengers killed in the United States is less than half that. Why, then, do rail crashes make headlines? Because since the first railways in the 1820s, the media has loved to cover train wrecks. The amount of media coverage devoted to railway accidents greatly outweighs the dangers of railway travel.

Amtrak is popular. It carries more than 24 million passengers annually and its ridership has been gradually increasing since it began services in 1971. More importantly for its survival, Amtrak's ridership, employees, and enthusiasts are devoted to keeping it alive. When riding Amtrak, it's not difficult to find crewmembers with more than 10 years' experience. Amtrak supporters also demonstrate a high level of devotion. Take David Clinton of Hingham, Massachusetts, who in the past 33 years has ridden virtually every Amtrak route "except the Florida trains and *Sunset*. I haven't done those, yet." His enthusiasm for Amtrak is unabashed: since 1972, David's car has carried the vanity Massachusetts license plate "AMTRAK."

In addition, Amtrak offers quality long-distance transport to those who cannot or choose not to drive. Ciara Dawson, from Ireland, has the unusual

Amtrak enjoys enormous popular support, but if its support fades, so will its trains. The *Southwest Chief* racing for Chicago blitzes the old semaphores at Model, Colorado, in September 1998. *Brian Solomon*

Amtrak *San Joaquin* No. 721 passes Pinole, California, on its way to Oakland. For a few years Amtrak assigned F40PHs and Horizon cars to this run. Today, F59PHI or GE P30BWHs with California cars are the norm. *Brian Solomon*

experience of traveling around the United States by Amtrak, having never seen the country by other means. She has traveled by train in many countries and found Amtrak very favorable by comparison. On Amtrak she traveled by coach on the *Crescent, Sunset Limited, Coast Starlight,* and *California Zephyr* (*CZ*). "Going by train is ideal," Dawson observed. "You can observe the passing countryside, cities, deserts, whatever without worrying about keeping your eyes on the road. You could sit there all day long taking in the passing [scenery]." She found Amtrak trains very clean, comfortable, and uniform and especially liked the big windows on Superliner Sightseer lounge cars. Her favorite ride was over Donner Pass on the *CZ*. "I was pretty excited about this journey because of the Donner Pass story."

It is my hope that readers of this book will gain a better understanding of Amtrak's history, its operations, equipment, and the service it provides. Although I explore Amtrak's challenges, explain the political motivations that have influenced Amtrak's direction, and investigate technical problems that have developed with some equipment, it is not my intent to offer specific criticisms of Amtrak, its management, employees, or its equipment manufacturers. Nor do I intend to offer detailed suggestions of how to reform, improve, or restructure Amtrak. These are topics that other authors have investigated at length.

There is certainly room for improvement with America's intercity railroad passenger system, but to address this issue fairly, one must look much deeper than merely criticizing

difficulties with day-to-day operations. America gets what it pays for. Nations with the best intercity railway networks have had a clear railway transport policy and over decades have made enormous investments in their basic railway infrastructure. This investment has paid off handsomely. It is unrealistic to expect that sexy technological solutions can quickly achieve the same long-term transportation solutions as long-term planning and investment.

In the present transport climate, Amtrak cannot be expected to achieve much more than what it already has achieved. To provide a world-class rail service, it is necessary to plan and invest in necessary rail infrastructure for years in advance of implementation.

Amtrak has demonstrated that investment in corridor services, for example, works. Ridership figures on Amtrak's corridor services have frequently exceeded projections. The keys to developing successful intercity passenger services are improved frequencies, regular-interval timings, faster schedules, and integrated support services, including clean user-friendly stations, safe public parking, and convenient public transit connections. As the costs of highway and air transport continue to rise, the demand for rail service will become more pressing. Hopefully, America will refocus its transport policy to fund Amtrak expansion and improvement. In the meantime Amtrak provides the best service it can, given very limited resources.

On the rear of the eastward *California Zephyr* **are Amtrak's Express Trak boxcars, used for hauling priority freight. In the late 1990s, Amtrak hoped to achieve self-sufficiency by subsidizing its passenger trains through the movement of high-value freight. New Amtrak President David Gunn opted out of this strategy when he learned that freight was costing Amtrak more than it was earning.** *Brian Solomon*

Amtrak ushered in a new era in American long-distance railway travel. In its first few years, Amtrak reversed declining intercity ridership and demonstrated that long-distance trains still had a future in American transport. In December 1989, Amtrak's eastward *California Zephyr* ascends Southern Pacific's crossing of Donner Pass, east of Alta, California, near the old timetable location of Gorge. Here, the tracks are more than 2,000 feet higher than the American River. *Brian Solomon*

CHAPTER ONE

RAILROADING: THE WAY FORWARD

The advent of the steam railroad revolutionized transportation. With the building of railroads, transit time between cities was cut from days to hours. Railroads made it easier, faster, and most important, cheaper to travel. They also created new transportation arteries and new towns where none had existed before. Whole metropolises, such as Chicago, grew up around important railroad junctions and

On an afternoon in June 1961, three Burlington E7 diesels depart Chicago Union Station with the westward *California Zephyr*. The original *CZ* was a privately run luxury dome liner connecting Chicago with California's Bay Area. Sadly, it made its final runs in 1970, the year before Amtrak assumed most American intercity passenger services. From the end of World War II until Amtrak, railroad passenger travel had experienced a precipitous decline and many famous trains were discontinued. *Richard Jay Solomon*

yards. The railroads facilitated the rapid settlement of the American West and allowed for the development, dispersion, and decentralization of American industry. America owes its unprecedented industrial and global political ascendancy to the fact that, in its formative years, it developed its resources quickly and efficiently. Railroads eased the tapping of those resources and the movement of products to market.

Beginning in the late 1820s, the American railroad network was largely built and operated by private, for-profit companies. Railroad construction occurred in frantic spurts throughout the nineteenth century, and by 1890 most of the route structure was in place. There was very little new route construction after the onset of World War I, and railroad mileage reached its zenith in the 1920s.

William E. Thoms explains in his book, *Reprieve for the Iron Horse*, that privately run railroads were in effect "quasi-public" companies afforded special privileges such as the power of eminent domain and protection from competition. In exchange for the right to take land and build their lines, railroads were given the legal and moral responsibilities to

Top: New York Central's premier passenger train was its New York City-Chicago *20th Century Limited*. In its heyday, the *20th Century* was an exclusive all-sleeping car train on an extra-fast express schedule. It was one of the best-known passenger trains in the world and a symbol of modern American railroading. Rather than allow the train to deteriorate, New York Central discontinued it in 1967 and America lost one of its transportation jewels. This view of the New York-bound *Century* was exposed along the Hudson near Manitou, New York, in the early 1960s. *Richard Jay Solomon*

Bottom: In the 1930s, the Pennsylvania Railroad electrified its heavily traveled New York City–Washington, D.C., route using a high-voltage AC overhead system. It was the most intensive electrification in the world at the time. The mainstays of PRR's passenger fleet were 139 GG1 electrics built between 1934 and 1935. In 1961, GG1 4924 leads a Washington-bound passenger train on the High Line in the Jersey Meadows. Today, this route is operated as Amtrak's Northeast Corridor. *Richard Jay Solomon*

The *California Zephyr* was one of America's favorite streamliners, operating daily between Chicago and Oakland and traversing the Burlington, Rio Grande, and Western Pacific railroads. One of the scenic highlights of the trip was Western Pacific's beautiful Feather River Canyon in the California Sierra. In 1968, the eastward *CZ* negotiates the famous Williams Loop, where the tracks make a full spiral to gain elevation near Spring Garden, California. The original *CZ* was discontinued in 1970, but Amtrak's modern train of the same name began in 1983 and crosses Donner Pass instead of the Feather River route. *Bob Morris*

provide common carrier freight transportation and to operate passenger trains in the
communities they served.

In some instances passenger traffic was
marginally profitable but much less lucrative
than freight revenue, so most American railroads
built their infrastructure to accommodate
freight traffic. Yet, some railroads, particularly
those in the East, earned a considerable portion
of their revenue from passenger business and
competed fiercely for passenger traffic. They
developed their infrastructures accordingly. The
New York Central (NYC), Pennsylvania (PRR),
and New Haven railroads were among the
largest passenger carriers.

Regulation, Competition, and Perception

By the twentieth century, federal and state
authorities regulated passenger traffic, making
it difficult for railroads to alter tariffs or train
frequencies and nearly impossible to eliminate
routes entirely.

However, following World War I, American
railroads began to face serious competition.
Over the succeeding decades the railroads'
supremacy was gradually eroded, first by highway
then by airline competition. These challenges
were facilitated by massive government investment in highways and airports. The nation's
traffic grew, but the railroads lost market
share in both freight and passenger businesses.

Decades of monopoly had made some
railroad companies wealthy, but had also
fostered deep public resentment due to real and
perceived abuses by those companies. This
resulted in a tide of railroad regulations
beginning in 1887 with the creation of
the Interstate Commerce Commission (ICC).
While undoubtedly some regulation was
needed, over-regulation gradually strangled
the industry in the succeeding decades.

The temporary nationalization of railroad
operations that coincided with American
involvement in World War I was another crucial
event in the industry. During this period, the

"Santa Fe All the Way"
was the railroad's
popular slogan. Santa
Fe's Alco-GE–built PA
diesel-electric No. 75
leads the eastward *San
Francisco Chief* over
the Western Pacific
crossing at Stockton,
California, in 1961.
Santa Fe was one of 17
railroads that joined
Amtrak in 1971 and
contributed the more
than $21 million in
buy-in fees required for
Amtrak to assume its
passenger services.
Today, Amtrak's *San
Joaquin*s use the old
Santa Fe route between
Port Chicago and
Bakersfield, California.
Bob Morris

Baltimore & Ohio was one railroad that did not allow the quality of its passenger services to deteriorate. In the 1960s, B&O's Paul Reistrup tried innovative ideas, such as playing feature films on board, to lure passengers back to the railroad. Ridership continued to decline, nevertheless. B&O's *Capitol Limited* is eastbound near Chicago on April 24, 1971, one week before the start of Amtrak operations would result in its discontinuance. Amtrak revived the *Capitol Limited* in 1981. *John Gruber*

railroads were bogged down with the surge of traffic to port cities from which troops and supplies embarked for Europe. These problems were compounded by interline rivalries and operational inefficiency, so Congress created the United States Railroad Administration to get things moving again. After the wartime crisis, the railroads were reluctantly returned to private control. Railroad management had soured toward government intervention in their businesses and, as a result, did not lobby to share in growing government investment in transportation infrastructure, which instead went to rival modes. One major exception was federal loans provided to the PRR in the 1930s to complete its New York–Washington–Harrisburg electrification.

The Passenger Conundrum

Strict rate regulation, tough labor protection, and competition aided by publicly funded

infrastructure, combined with public animosity toward railroads, resulted in stagnation and decline, a general trend partly masked by the unprecedented surge in traffic during World War II.

Weakened by the Great Depression and competition from highways, the railroads were hit hard in the postwar years. Their plant had been pounded by enormous traffic and suffered from years of deferred maintenance. Passenger traffic and revenue dropped off precipitously as Americans bought automobiles and ever more highways were built. Despite regulatory hurdles, railroads curtailed passenger services as quickly as permitted. The number of daily intercity passenger trains operated nationally shrunk from about 20,000 on the eve of the Depression in 1929 to just 420 in 1970. The railroads went from the dominant form of intercity passenger transport to marginal players in what was

generally a growing business. America went from having one of the best passenger networks in the world to the worst of all industrialized countries.

Many railroads had introduced high-speed streamlined trains in the 1930s and, in the postwar economy, hoped to capitalize on their great wartime boom in passenger traffic. The goal was illusory, but the companies at first invested heavily in new diesels and streamlined passenger trains. Yet, traffic continued to drop. By the mid-1950s, railroads finally realized that unsubsidized passenger services were doomed. The economics of operating trains had changed and most passenger services went from being marginally profitable to vastly unprofitable. The federally funded Interstate highway system made the plight of intercity rail services even more desperate. The end of all passenger service was predicted, by the late 1950s. The few attempts made to introduce

low-cost, lightweight trains had failed, and in 1958 Congress made it easier to cut services. Over the next decade, many of America's best-known trains made their final runs, and many railroads deliberately allowed their services to deteriorate. By the mid-1960s, poorly maintained stations and trains were contributing to a further loss of ridership.

Another factor that contributed to the decline of the passenger train was the decline of American cities. The suburbanization of America was not conducive to traditional intercity railway travel, and the railways were both unwilling and incapable of investing in new infrastructure to cater to a new generation of dispersed passengers. Railroad stations traditionally served downtown areas, and as those districts became unfashionable and fell into decay, going to the station became undesirable. Hotels near railroad stations, once among the finest in the country, became

The fledgling Amtrak's first new equipment was a pair of RTG Turboliners imported from France in 1973. Powercar No. 59, pictured in Milwaukee, Wisconsin, on January 21, 1977, was part of the second order for ANF-Frangeco Turboliners delivered in 1975. The RTG turbos were initially assigned to Midwest runs originating in Chicago. *John Gruber*

A pair of brand-new SDP40Fs leads Amtrak's eastward *San Francisco Zephyr* across the Carquinez Straits at Benecia, California, in 1974. Southern Pacific opened this enormous bridge—the largest double-track railroad bridge west of the Mississippi—in 1930. Prior to that, trains were floated across the straits between Benecia and Port Costa. Today, it is on the route of the *California Zephyr*, *Coast Starlight*, and *Capitol*s. *Bob Morris*

seedy and unsavory. Urban transit systems similarly declined and retrenched. As ridership declined and service deteriorated, operating costs became increasingly burdensome.

A few lines, such as the Northern Pacific, Santa Fe, Baltimore & Ohio, and Southern Railway, continued to maintain their flagship trains to high standards, both as a matter of company pride and to provide excellent advertising tools. Other railroads sought to exit the business completely.

Then, in 1967, the U.S. Postal Service chose not to renew most railroad mail contracts. Prior to this time, the mail was a staple of revenue on most intercity passenger trains. This announcement doomed even more trains, causing Santa Fe, for example, to slash its schedules and NYC to drop its legendary *20th Century Limited*.

Government Aid

In 1958, the city of Philadelphia became among the first to provide public subsidy for regional suburban services when it set up the Passenger Service Improvement Corporation to provide relief for Reading's and PRR's commuter operations.

In 1962, U.S. Senator Claiborne Pell of Rhode Island introduced a bill to modernize railway services between Boston and Washington, D.C. Congress' interest in improving service in the Northeast was further advanced by the enormous public success of the Japanese Shinkansen, which opened in 1964. This all-new railway system used high-speed, electrically powered "bullet trains" to move large numbers of passengers between Tokyo and Osaka. The train's design was essentially a refinement of American technology developed for the Pennsylvania and New Haven railroads in the 1920s and 1930s. The Europeans were also advancing high-speed railway technology; the French had tested electric locomotives at speeds faster than 200 miles per hour.

In September 1965, Congress passed the High Speed Ground Transportation Act, which resulted in development of the Budd-built Metroliner electric multiple unit and United Aircraft's TurboTrain for high-speed service on the Northeast Corridor (NEC).

A pair of E8s leads Amtrak's *National Limited* through a rock cut near Kirkwood, Missouri, in 1973. Both E8s were conveyed to Amtrak by Penn Central, and the trailing locomotive, No. 309, still wears black PC paint. Both were off the roster within two years, having been displaced by new SDP40Fs. The *National Limited* operated between New York and Kansas City, Missouri, with a connection to Washington, D.C. This was one of several runs discontinued with the autumn 1979 timetable change. *Bob Morris*

Penn Central had the highest passenger deficits and thus the most to gain by joining Amtrak. Among its contributions were hundreds of locomotives, cars, and other equipment. The early Amtrak-era on PC lines looked much like Penn Central-era passenger operations. On April 7, 1973, Amtrak train No. 74, led by former PC E8A 259 with former PC cars, overtakes an eastward freight at Chili, New York. One clue that this is an Amtrak train is the E8A's road number—as a PC unit, it had been No. 4041. *Doug Eisele*

Financial Woes Urge Action

The PRR and NYC had been two of the largest and traditionally the most powerful railroads in the United States. In 1968, they merged, following years of complex negotiations and regulatory proceedings. It was a belated effort to reduce the redundancy of the railroads' overlapping systems and avert financial collapse. A regulatory condition of the merger compelled the new Penn Central (PC) to take on the bankrupt New Haven in January 1969. Unfortunately, PC was poorly conceived and the merger badly executed, which acceler-

ated, rather than averted, the company's financial deterioration.

The failure of PC had direct implications in the creation of Amtrak. PC was by far the largest rail passenger carrier in the United States, but because PC was sustaining substantial passenger losses, it was desperate to be rid of this burden. Most American railroads wanted out of passenger business so they could focus on freight, but PC's case was extreme. By this time, growing political support for the preservation of American intercity passenger services was putting pressure on Congress to take action.

Railpax

In the late 1960s, Congress and the newly created U.S. Department of Transportation (DOT) worked to find an acceptable government solution to two distinct passenger-rail problems: to relieve the railroads of their passenger burden as quickly and as painlessly as possible and to

preserve a core passenger-rail network and curb the decline in ridership.

Senator Vance Hartke of Indiana, chairman of the Senate Transportation Subcommittee, favored legislation that would provide direct subsidy to privately operated rail services. This plan was not politically acceptable. Thoms quotes DOT Undersecretary James M. Beggs as saying in 1969:

> In particular, the creation of a Federal operating subsidy for rail passenger service . . . creates a serious risk that the Government will become entangled in an undertaking that will increasingly burden the taxpayer without providing adequate relief to the nation's railroads. Operating subsidies, as experience with other government programs has shown, are at best a palliative.

Another idea discussed at the time was a federal agency to operate passenger trains.

May 1, 1971, was the low point in American intercity passenger train route miles. Shortly after Amtrak assumed operation of the nation's long-distance trains it started adding new routes and restored service between Oakland and Bakersfield, California, in 1974 with its *San Joaquin*. Train No. 711 was photographed at the end of its run at Oakland's 16th Street Station on July 16, 1976. This train often ran with former Southern Pacific FP7s, such as 377 and 376, pictured here. They had been SP 6454 and 6453, respectively. *Brian Jennison*

This seemed like the best solution, but it presented serious logistical hurdles. There had been no precedent for government operation of rail service on privately owned lines since World War I. Furthermore, there was great fear in the industry that government passenger operation was just the first step toward total railroad nationalization. (By the late 1960s, America's privately operated railways were an anomaly. In the rest of the world, railways and railway companies were, in one form or another, under state control with heavy government subsidies.) To overcome

On August 5, 1974, New York Governor Malcolm Wilson cuts the ribbon on the opening day for the new Amtrak *Adirondack* at the Albany-Rensselaer Station. Initially this train used Delaware & Hudson equipment that New York State paid to rehabilitate. *Jim Shaughnessy*

The inaugural of Amtrak's *Adirondack* on August 5, 1974, at Albany-Rensselaer, New York. Using Delaware & Hudson's famous Alco-GE–built PA diesels and classy traditional passenger cars, in its early days the *Adirondack* was a throwback to the heyday of the American streamliner. Without question, it was one of the most attractive trains Amtrak has ever run. *Jim Shaughnessy*

A rebuilt Delaware & Hudson passenger car for service on the *Adirondack*. *Jim Shaughnessy*

Two streamliner designs separated by nearly 30 years: Delaware & Hudson's former Santa Fe Alco-GE PA No. 16 sits across the platform from a nearly new Rohr Turboliner at Albany-Rensselaer on February 10, 1977. The PA diesel was designed by General Electric's Raymond E. Patten and introduced in 1946. The Rohr Turboliner debuted in 1976. Amtrak used D&H's PAs on the *Adirondack* between 1974 and 1977. *Jim Shaughnessy*

Passengers wait for Amtrak's *Empire Builder* at Columbus, Wisconsin, on June 19, 1976. The *Empire Builder*, trains 7 and 8, operate from Chicago to St. Paul over the old Milwaukee Road, now part of Canadian Pacific. The remainder of the trip largely uses the former Great Northern line, now operated by Burlington Northern Santa Fe. GN's founder was the legendary James J. Hill, known as the "Empire Builder." *John Gruber*

these fears, a "quasi-public" passenger rail corporation, favored by the Nixon administration, was suggested. It would not be a government agency, but rather a for-profit corporation controlled by the government. Following these guidelines, DOT, under the direction of Transportation Secretary John A. Volpe, drafted plans for the National Railroad Passenger Corporation (NRPC), known colloquially in its formative state as Railpax. (Thoms notes that Railpax is the telegraphic symbol for railroad passenger, and that the name, as applied to this formative federal passenger rail corporation, is credited to Paul Cherington, then a professor at the Massachusetts Institute of Technology.)

National Railroad Passenger Corporation

On January 18, 1970, DOT announced its Railpax plan that was to "be patterned after

the Communication Satellite Corporation—the quasi-public corporation that operated telecommunications satellites," according to an article by Robert Lindsey in the *New York Times*. Railpax's routes were yet to be determined by DOT.

As Railpax was debated, Penn Central's woes were getting worse. In March 1970, PC petitioned the ICC to discontinue all of its passenger services west of Buffalo, New York, and Harrisburg, Pennsylvania, which would have effectively ended passenger service between most eastern cities and the Midwest. In May, Railpax legislation was introduced in the Senate; it passed in June. That month, PC declared bankruptcy, the largest in history up to that time.

The Penn Central collapse rocked Wall Street, and the House of Representatives introduced a more generous Railpax plan. As the railroad rotted, the politicians debated. Finally

Above: The *Empire Builder* arrives at Columbus, Wisconsin, on June 19, 1976. In the consist are several Budd-built Vistadomes. Today, this train runs with Superliners. *John Gruber*

Conductor J. S. Lawson collects a ticket from Richard Gruber at Superior, Wisconsin, on July 26, 1976. *John Gruber*

In addition to its regularly scheduled trains, Amtrak operates a variety of special trains. On September 25, 1976, Amtrak P30CH 701 leads a football special from Milwaukee to Madison, Wisconsin, down Milwaukee Road's line on East Main Street in Madison. The cars are former Chicago & North Western bi-level commuter equipment that Amtrak used on short- to medium-distance services in the Midwest. *John Gruber*

in October, both the House and Senate passed improved legislation creating the NRPC. There were fears that Railpax would die on the president's desk. Some of President Richard Nixon's advisors were publicly against the plan, but apparently Nixon himself had a soft spot for trains. Frank Wilner, in his book *The Amtrak Story*, cites Nixon's memoirs in which the president explained that "all through grade school my ambition was to become a railroad engineer."

Nixon's motives were not just personal. At the time, difficulties with the Vietnam War were causing great public controversy and Nixon didn't want to generate more negative publicity for the White House by giving the American passenger train a public execution. On October 29, 1970, he signed the Railpax legislation, known as the Rail Passenger Service Act of 1970.

The purposes of the act were summarized:

To provide financial assistance for and establishment of a national rail passenger system, to provide for the modernization of railroad passenger equipment, to authorize the prescribing of minimum standards for railroad passenger service, to amend section 13a of the Interstate Commerce Act [outlining legal procedures for discontinuing rail passenger services], and for other purposes.

Among other things, the Rail Passenger Service Act forever changed the methods for train discontinuance, and Railpax temporarily froze all efforts to discontinue trains, while DOT worked out a final system plan. At that time, 59 of the remaining 421 passenger trains running in the United States were pending discontinuance before the ICC.

Under the Rail Passenger Service Act, railroads could either both join Railpax and provide it with cash, equipment, or the equivalent, or stay out of it. If they opted out, they would be obligated to operate passenger services at existing levels until 1975, at which time they could apply for discontinuance.

Lines that joined would be immediately free of long-distance passenger obligations and have the choice of receiving either NPRC common stock or a tax write-off. Section 101 of the act reads:

The Congress finds that modern, efficient, intercity railroad passenger service is a necessary part of a balanced transportation system; that the public convenience and necessity require the continuance and improvement of such service to provide fast and comfortable transportation between crowded urban areas and in other areas of the country; that rail passenger service can help to end the congestion on our highways and the overcrowding of airways and airports; that the traveler in America should to the maximum extent feasible have the freedom to choose the mode of travel most convenient to his needs; that to achieve these goals requires the designation of a basic national rail passenger system and the establishment of a rail passenger corporation for the purpose of providing modern, efficient, intercity rail passenger service; that Federal financial assistance as well as investment capital from the private sector of the economy is needed for this purpose; and that Federal financial assistance to certain railroads may be necessary to permit the orderly transfer of railroad passenger service to a railroad passenger corporation.

The act goes on to specifically define intercity rail passenger service as follows:

. . . all rail passenger service other than (A) commuter and other short-haul service in metropolitan and suburban areas, usually characterized by reduced fare, multiple-ride and commutation tickets, and by morning and evening peak period

Amtrak dome observation car 9310 brings up the tail of the *Arrowhead* at Superior, Wisconsin, in October 1977. Amtrak began the Minneapolis-Duluth, Minnesota *Arrowhead* in April 1975. The train name was changed to the *North Star* in April 1978 in conjunction with the addition of a through sleeper to Chicago. The sleeper was dropped in October 1981, and the *North Star* was discontinued in October 1986. *Steve Smedley*

Amtrak No. 48, the *Lake Shore Limited*, passes Anthony's Nose along the Hudson River near Peekskill, New York, on October 15, 1976. In the background is the Bear Mountain Bridge, which often featured in advertisements for New York Central's famed *20th Century Limited*. At Harmon, New York, this pair of E8As will be exchanged for an FL9 for the run into Grand Central Terminal. *George Kowanski*

operations, and (B) auto-ferry service characterized by transportation of automobiles and their occupants where contracts for such service have been consummated prior to enactment of this Act.

Thus, most commuter rail operations were outside the scope of Amtrak. (Definition B referred to the original Auto-Train, a private company that had a contract with host railroads to operate between Virginia and Florida.)

The passenger train that had once been the dominant form of intercity transport was saved from extinction to offer alternative transport in the face of growing highway and airport congestion. The Rail Passenger Service Act not only saved the intercity passenger train, but also revealed America's primary transport agenda. Simultaneous with the creation of the NRPC, the already massive funding for highways and airports was accelerated.

Drafting a Final System Plan

Secretary Volpe and DOT had until November 30, 1970, to draft the basic Railpax route plan. It was expected that only a portion of existing rail routes would be retained under Railpax operations. Some lines would be saved, while others would be altered, and a great many cut.

The Rail Passenger Service Act stated that while the NRPC was "for-profit," it required federal financial assistance and made provision for limited startup funding. However, financing over the long term was not clarified and limited capital placed tight constraints on the design of a national system. Furthermore, DOT was given little more than a month to draft its Basic System Plan. Thoms explains Volpe's strategy:

> Improving the quality of service is essential to reverse ridership trends. Available funds should be concentrated on a limited

On December 17, 1977, Amtrak's northward *Floridian* makes its station stop at Louisville, Kentucky, with SDP40F 607 in the lead. The train was running eight hours late as a result of a detour via Evansville, Indiana, due to a freight train derailment in Bowling Green, Kentucky. Upon reaching Evansville, the train then had to backtrack eastward along the south bank of the Ohio River in order to reach Louisville. Amtrak's *Floridian* was one of several trains axed in 1979, and Amtrak has been without a direct Chicago-Florida train ever since. *Brian Jennison*

number of routes that show some promise of profitability so that improvements can be made.

In selecting routes, the emphasis should be on realistic projections of future demand and costs.

Even though funds should be concentrated on a limited number of routes, route selection should provide a basic system on which service can be added if response is favorable.

DOT studied ridership patterns, determined which cities ought to retain rail service and which could afford to lose it, and considered which routes were most suitable. Wilner writes that Volpe predicted Railpax would break even after three years and emerge to sustain profitability. This belief was contrary to voluminous evidence presented by American railroads and by railways around the world, which demonstrated that rail passenger service cannot exist without some sort of subsidy. Virtually no one in the American railroad industry believed that passenger service could be made profitable.

The Nixon administration had its own agenda. While the president had endorsed the creation of Railpax, members of his administration fought Volpe's route plans. The White House wanted Railpax to focus on high-density East Coast routes serving the largest markets. Volpe wanted to develop a more balanced system reaching across the nation.

These two views depict Amtrak's southward *Adirondack* train 68, at the same location on the Delaware & Hudson near Port Henry. On August 15, 1975, D&H PA 19 does the honors. *Jim Shaughnessy*

Political pressures urged the inclusion of West Coast routes, such as Southern Pacific's *Sunset, Coast,* and *Shasta* routes that Volpe had initially excluded. The final system plan, adopted by Railpax, and ultimately implemented on May 1, 1971, included the following basic routes:

- The Northeast Corridor: Boston–Washington, D.C., and connecting service to Springfield, Massachusetts;
- Empire Service: New York (Grand Central)–Albany–Buffalo;
- New York (Penn Station)–Chicago via Philadelphia, Pittsburgh, and Ft. Wayne, Indiana, with connecting service to Washington, D.C.;
- New York City–Kansas City, Missouri;
- New York–Florida routes to Miami and Tampa/St. Petersburg;
- Chicago Midwestern services, connecting this traditional hub with Milwaukee, Detroit, Cincinnati, and St. Louis;
- Chicago–Miami via Louisville, Kentucky, and Birmingham, Alabama;
- Chicago–New Orleans;
- Chicago–Houston via Kansas City, Missouri, and Oklahoma City;
- Chicago–Los Angeles;
- Chicago–Oakland, California;
- Chicago–Seattle;
- Newport News, Virginia–Cincinnati via Charlottesville, Virginia, with connection to Washington, D.C., from Charlottesville;

• New Orleans–Los Angeles; and
• San Diego–Los Angeles–Seattle.
Outside of the Northeast, most routes were served by just one roundtrip daily, and several key western routes were proposed to have just tri-weekly service.

Because DOT anticipated Denver & Rio Grande Western and Southern Railway would join Railpax, initial plans included running the Chicago–Oakland service over the Rio Grande system between Denver and Salt Lake City and operating Southern's New York–Washington, D.C.–Atlanta–New Orleans *Crescent* route. However, these were among the abstaining railroads that continued to operate their own trains. Southern ultimately joined the NRPC in 1979, Rio Grande joined in 1983.

Experimental and State-Sponsored Service

Railpax was never limited to basic service. Section 403 of the act lists several types of new services that could be provided beyond the Basic System Plan. Section 403(a) states:

The Corporation may provide intercity rail passenger service in excess of that prescribed for the basic system, either within or outside the basic system, including the operation of special and extra passenger trains, if consistent with prudent management. Any intercity rail passenger service provided under this subsection for a continuous period of two years shall be designated by the Secretary as a part of the basic system.

On May 7, 1977, the *Adirondack* comprises a Rohr Turboliner. After being bumped from Amtrak No. 68 and 69, Delaware & Hudson's four PA diesels worked in Massachusetts Bay Transit Authority commuter service out of Boston for a few months before being sold to Mexico. Two PAs have since been repatriated and are under restoration by Doyle McCormack in Oregon. *Jim Shaughnessy*

Amtrak's first southward *Palmetto* changes crews at Florence, South Carolina, on June 15, 1976. Photographer Doug Riddell explains, "Believe it or not, I was riding with Rogers Whitaker [*The New Yorker* writer E. M. Frimbo]. The train was *so* far ahead of schedule that Amtrak Vice President David Watts had the *Palmetto* halted out of sight for several minutes, just north of the depot at Florence, to avoid any appearance that the running time was padded. In truth, it wasn't. [Seaboard Coast Line] engineers simply were legendary for using their operating skills to insure on-time performance. What the photo doesn't reflect is the crew's perplexity at being scolded, in effect, for doing *too* good a job that day." *Doug Riddell*

Section 403(b) states: "Any State, regional, or local agency may request of the Corporation rail passenger service beyond that included with the basic system. The Corporation shall institute such service if the State, regional, or local agency agrees to reimburse the Corporation for a reasonable portion of any losses associated with such services."

Section 403(b) thus allowed states and regional authorities to expand services. Within days of the NRPC's first runs, 403(b) was invoked to expand service to regions not included in the Basic System Plan.

Amtrak

Today, Amtrak is one of the oldest railroad companies in the United States operating under the same name with which it started. Nearly all of the operators that conveyed their passenger services to Amtrak in 1971 have since disappeared as a result of mergers and corporate restructuring. With this perspective, it may seem inconceivable that the Amtrak name was coined only weeks before it was to assume operation of most intercity passenger services in the United States.

Why "Amtrak"? The National Railroad Passenger Corporation was too cumbersome for everyday usage, and some people feared that Railpax was too easily corruptible, so the New York public relations firm Lippincott and Margulies was hired to come up with something better. By blending "America" and "track" (some sources say they blended America, travel, and track), they coined the now-familiar name. In addition, Lippincott and Margulies designed Amtrak's first corporate herald, the famous "pointless arrow." On April 21, 1971, Railpax disappeared from the railroad lexicon, and Amtrak has stood for America's long-distance passenger services ever since.

On April 28, 1971, just four days before Amtrak was to begin service, Roger Lewis, a former vice president at Pan American Airways and former president of General Dynamics, was appointed as its first president. On May 1, with its small budget, its fresh name and logo, and a handful of employees, Amtrak began operations. In the hours that passed between April 30 and May 1, half the remaining passenger trains in the United States made their final runs. At its inaugural, Amtrak was responsible for running just 184 daily intercity trains, the majority of which operated in the Northeast. Initially, 17 railroads signed contracts with Amtrak: Burlington

The Amtrak departure and arrival board at San Diego, California, in 1978. *Fred Matthews*

Against the backdrop of the Connecticut capitol building, a Springfield, Massachusetts-bound train approaches the station at Hartford on November 26, 1988. At that time, the New Haven-Springfield line was operated as traditional direction double-track. Amtrak has since reduced the line to a single-track operation under centralized traffic control and upgraded the remaining main track with heavy continuous welded rail. *Brian Solomon*

Northern; Baltimore & Ohio/ Chesapeake & Ohio; Chicago & North Western; Delaware & Hudson; Grand Trunk Western; Gulf, Mobile & Ohio; Illinois Central; Louisville & Nashville; Milwaukee Road; Missouri Pacific; Norfolk & Western; Penn Central; Richmond, Fredericksburg & Potomac; Santa Fe; Seaboard Coast Line; Southern Pacific; and Union Pacific. Of these, Chicago & North Western, Delaware & Hudson, Grand Trunk Western, and Norfolk & Western did not initially host Amtrak trains. Today, of those 17 railroads, the only one still operating with its name intact is Union Pacific. Delaware & Hudson (D&H) also exists but is operated as part of Canadian Pacific.

Dawn or Sunset?

Amtrak was not a railroad in the traditional sense. It owned neither the routes nor the tracks on which it operated. It didn't employ operating crews—they were supplied by Amtrak's host railroads and paid for by Amtrak. Even most of its equipment was leased from the joining lines.

When Lewis took the helm of Amtrak he was unknown to the railroad industry. His only railroad experience was that his father had worked for a railroad. Wilner relates that Lewis was offered the job of president so suddenly that he fumbled the name of the company in his first press conference, announcing that he was "pleased to be the new president of Ampax."

A New Haven, Connecticut-bound shuttle from Springfield, Massachusetts, crosses the stone arch bridge at Windsor, Connecticut, in November 1988. *Brian Solomon*

Denver & Rio Grande Western was the last private railroad in the United States to operate its own long-distance passenger service, running its tri-weekly *Rio Grande Zephyr* until 1983. Rio Grande initially stayed out of Amtrak because it didn't want another operator's passenger trains interfering with its freight schedules. The eastward *RGZ* ascends Soldier Summit, Utah. *Mel Patrick*

Despite its abrupt beginning and lack of public name recognition, Amtrak supporters had high hopes for the corporation. It had a congressional mandate to improve railroad passenger service, and it hoped to fulfill its promise. In a March 1974 interview in *Railway Gazette International,* Lewis explained that in its first two years Amtrak had improved the quality of service assumed from more than a dozen different carriers. It simplified fare structures and lowered many fares to attract passengers. It allowed customers to purchase tickets using a variety of credit cards. And it standardized baggage-carrying arrangements, introduced creative marketing, and improved schedules.

Consolidating passenger services gave Amtrak the opportunity to make several basic improvements by integrating once privately operated services. Prior to Amtrak, most passenger services in the United States were not operated as a unified system. Each company operated its own trains and usually served its own stations. Although there were instances of through trains and through cars operated by two or more railroads, as well as "union stations" in some cities serving multiple railroads, in many cases lines did not coordinate schedules. One of the few examples of a unified service prior to Amtrak was the sleeping-car network traditionally offered by the Pullman Company, which had provided

sleepers on virtually every railroad in North America, offering through overnight services between most major cities. However, these services too had been assumed by the individual railroads prior to Amtrak.

In addition to coordinating schedules, Amtrak introduced computerized ticketing and reservations, making the purchase of through tickets much easier. Amtrak also set up centralized reservation centers, the first opening in April 1973 at Bensalem, Pennsylvania. Amtrak quickly culled the worse passenger cars from its fleet, ultimately retaining just 1,200 of the 3,000 cars originally transferred to the corporation.

Amtrak Grows

Volpe's Basic System Plan left out some politically popular routes. On May 10, 1971, Amtrak began operating its first service under the 403(b) clause, the *Lake Shore Limited* between New York (Grand Central), Albany, Buffalo, Cleveland, and Chicago. In its original incarnation, this service was short-lived and it was withdrawn in January 1972, but restored again in 1975. The Boston–Springfield–New Haven Inland Route was restored on May 17, 1971, with a train appropriately named the *Bay State*. Like the *Lake Shore Limited*, it too was relatively short-lived but later revived. A second Chicago–Seattle service was introduced June 5, 1971, with the *North*

The *Lake Shore Limited* makes its station stop at Rochester, New York, on March 30, 1988. Rochester is home to Eastman Kodak, whose office building can be seen on the left. Appropriately, this dawn image was exposed on Kodachrome 25 slide film. Train 48/448 typically carried a lot of mail, as evidenced by material handling cars located behind the locomotives. *Brian Solomon*

W. Graham Claytor Jr. was one of Amtrak's most dynamic leaders and ensured the railroad's survival through the difficult Reagan years. Claytor speaks at High Point, North Carolina, in October 1984 at the inaugural of the *Carolinian*. The initial *Carolinian* service between Charlotte, North Carolina, and New York City was a trial and was discontinued in the spring of 1985. The train became a permanent service in 1990, but its routing was longer as a result of the abandonment of the old Seaboard Air Line route north of Raleigh. *Doug Koontz*

boosted with the addition of a third roundtrip, and Amtrak introduced the *Illinois Zephyr* between Chicago and Quincy, Illinois.

Bowing to political pressure, Amtrak added even more routes in 1972. Like other new services, these each featured just a single daily roundtrip. In addition, Amtrak had been authorized to begin international services and introduced the Seattle–Vancouver, British Columbia, *Pacific International* in July and the Washington, D.C.–New York City–Montreal *Montrealer* service via a Vermont routing at the end of September. Senator Winston L. Prouty of Vermont had been an ardent supporter of Railpax during the planning process and was disappointed when the Final System Plan did not incorporate a Montreal service. Vermont had lost its last passenger services in September 1966, several years before Railpax planning, but the constituency of this state has had a long-standing passion for its trains and has supported them throughout Amtrak's history.

Funding Woes

Fears that Amtrak was underfunded quickly proved accurate. Only a few months after startup, Amtrak needed additional subsidies from Congress. The fact that Amtrak was never given a designated source of operating funds, combined with the political nature of its creation, route structure, and operation, has resulted in a cyclical crisis that has dogged the railroad since it began operations.

Aggravating Amtrak's plight has been its planners' unrealistic expectations that it could achieve and sustain profitability. While some individual trains may be deemed profitable, as a rule, when all costs are weighed, passenger networks are not prone to sustained profitability. Unfortunately, the lack of a designated funding source and the fact that highway and airport funding is appropriated differently (such as through the gasoline tax) and avoids the appearance of financial loss have given Amtrak's requests for its annual operating

Coast Hiawatha, which traversed the former Northern Pacific and served important cities missed by Amtrak's Chicago–Seattle *Empire Builder*, which follows the more northerly former Great Northern route. In November 1971, Los Angeles–San Diego service was

On Halloween 1983, Amtrak's inaugural southward *Auto Train* departs Lorton, Virginia, behind P30CH 707 and will head out on the Richmond, Fredericksburg & Potomac mainline. By morning it will be in Sanford, Florida. This auto-ferry passenger train has become one of Amtrak's premier services and one of the few trains that recovers more than its long-term costs. *Doug Koontz*

Amtrak assumed operation of Southern Railway's New York City-Atlanta-New Orleans *Crescent* on February 1, 1979. Southern merged with Norfolk & Western to form Norfolk Southern in 1982. On May 23, 1992, Norfolk Southern GP38-2 5057 and a pair of Amtrak F40PHs led the northward *Crescent*, train No. 20, near Lynchburg, Virginia. *Doug Koontz*

For many railroaders, the railroad is more than a job, it's a way of life, and it is not unusual to find Amtrak employees with decades of service. When Amtrak conductor Dick Meehan was photographed at Toledo, Ohio, on May 26, 1994, he was 74 years old and had 52 years of seniority. He started working for the Pennsylvania Railroad in 1941. *David Palmer*

subsidies and capital investments the appearance of bailouts. In reality, however, modern-day Amtrak does a much better job of recovering its expenses through fare collection than most passenger railways in the world. Amtrak's funding situation results in flawed perceptions that it does not fulfill its role and therefore represents wasted taxpayer money.

Wilner explains that between 1958 and 1971, when passenger trains were still privately run and when the ICC approved the discontinuance of most intercity trains, the federal government invested more than $50 billion to build and improve American highways, including the development of the Interstate system. Thanks to this massive investment, the highway industry evolved as one of the biggest businesses in America. Amtrak's yearly operating subsidies and capital improvements are miniscule compared to the total U.S. transportation subsidy.

The primary reason for Amtrak's service challenges is chronic underinvestment in its basic infrastructure. Amtrak's funding short-fall has been one of the dominant themes of

Denver Union Station once served trains of Rio Grande, Union Pacific, Burlington, Colorado & Southern, Santa Fe, and Rock Island. Today, Amtrak's daily *California Zephyr* is the only regular service there. The classic terminal is a fixture of downtown Denver. *Brian Solomon*

Englewood, Illinois, south of Chicago, was a famous railroad junction where the parallel New York Central and Pennsylvania Railroads crossed the Rock Island. January 2, 1995, dawned with sub-zero temperatures as Amtrak's Chicago-Toronto *International* crossed the old Rock at Englewood tower. This train often operated with a VIA Rail F40PH. VIA is Amtrak's Canadian equivalent, providing services on the Canadian National and Canadian Pacific railways. *Brian Solomon*

its existence. Its periodic funding crises are like professional wrestling—there are predictable fights with predictable results, but spectators find it interesting to watch anyway. During these times of national funding shortfalls, Amtrak becomes a public whipping post for government waste. Still, Amtrak's supporters have always ensured that it survives, yet it never thrives. Outside the Northeast Corridor, which is Amtrak's busiest route and its greatest success, most of its growth has been state-funded.

Middle East Crisis Boosts Amtrak

In its first two years, Amtrak succeeded in ending the free fall of intercity passenger ridership. In fact, in 1973, the number of train passengers rose slightly. It seemed that Amtrak might be successful after all.

Fears that Amtrak was little more than a government experiment and that its rail

operations would be quietly shut down after two years went away with the onset of the 1973 oil embargo. Nationwide shortages sent gasoline prices through the roof. Suddenly, Amtrak seemed to have a valid role in the future of American transportation. Expansion, rather than extinction, became the talk of the industry. President Nixon, embroiled in his own political troubles, signed the Amtrak Improvement Act in November 1973 and indicated that he felt rail travel was in America's national interest. Among the changes written in the act was a mandate that Amtrak introduce

When Paul Reistrup led Amtrak, Congress authorized Amtrak's purchase of the Northeast Corridor and provided funding to upgrade tracks, catenary, and signals. By 1977, work was under way. One of Amtrak's venerable former Pennsylvania Railroad GG1 electrics zips along with a "Clocker" at North Elizabeth, New Jersey. *Fred Matthews*

at least one new long-distance service every year, although this service could be dropped after two years if deemed unsuccessful.

Amtrak's Lewis optimistically stated in the March 1974 *Railway Gazette International*, "America's energy crisis has provided the final push needed to transform intercity rail travel from a holding operation into a growth industry." He further explained that the oil crisis gave Amtrak the capital it needed to purchase large fleets of new cars and locomotives, not just for its NEC, but for the entire system.

Over the next few years, Amtrak ordered new turbo trains, hundreds of new single-level Amfleet cars, bi-level Superliner cars, and hundreds of new diesel and electric locomotives. In part, this allowed for modest service expansion, but more importantly, it also allowed the replacement of much of the old, inherited "heritage" equipment, which was getting pretty tired. Amtrak was able to rebuild the best of its older equipment to modern standards.

During 1974 and 1975, Amtrak added new routes and trains, both as a result the 1973 Amtrak Improvement Act and with state assistance. On Valentine's Day 1974, the Chicago–Dubuque, Iowa *Black Hawk* debuted, using an Illinois Central Gulf routing across northern Illinois. In March, California's *San*

Sometimes circumstances beyond Amtrak's control complicate operations. In spring 1986, a labor action on the Boston & Maine forced Amtrak to implement a temporary detour for trains Nos. 60 and 61, the *Montrealer*. As a result, the trains used a Springfield-Palmer, Massachusetts, Conrail routing and the Central Vermont between Palmer and East Northfield to avoid a portion of B&M's Connecticut River Line. On March 16, 1986, No. 61 paused in front of the old station at Palmer to change directions necessitated by the movement from Conrail onto CV. Today, this is the normal route of Amtrak's daily *Vermonter*. *Brian Solomon*

Joaquin service between Oakland and Bakersfield was introduced. In August, New York State and Amtrak reintroduced service on the D&H to Montreal, initially using D&H's own passenger equipment. The *Blue Water* debuted in September between Chicago and Port Huron, Michigan, while New York (Grand Central)– Buffalo –Detroit service via Ontario began in October. Expansion in 1975 included additional service between Chicago and Detroit, an extension of the *Lone Star* to Dallas (one of the largest American cities that had gone without passenger service before Amtrak's creation), and the reintroduction of the *Lake Shore Limited*, including a Boston section.

New Management and New Opportunity

While Amtrak braced for growth as a result of the energy crisis, American freight railroading was undergoing a radical transformation that would affect Amtrak's operations. Following Penn Central's well-publicized financial collapse, a number of other Northeastern railroads also succumbed, forcing Congress to fund a

bailout. The result was the creation of Conrail in 1976.

In early 1975, Roger Lewis stepped down, and on March 1, Paul Reistrup assumed the presidency of Amtrak. Unlike Lewis, Reistrup had a strong railroad background, had excellent credentials in the passenger business, and was well respected in the industry. Reistrup had been in charge of passenger services at Baltimore & Ohio (B&O) and later at Illinois Central. At B&O from 1964 to 1966 he caught industry attention by trying a variety of innovative approaches to attract ridership at a time when passenger trains were largely viewed as a lost cause. Many considered him the top choice to run Amtrak.

The Penn Central debacle was a mixed blessing for Amtrak. The majority of Amtrak's trains operated over PC routes. The bankrupt carrier, however, had often been incapable of

maintaining tracks to acceptable standards. This caused rough-riding cars and innumerable delays. Further, much of the equipment inherited from PC suffered from years of poor maintenance and was largely worn out.

On the other hand, Amtrak benefited directly from the liquidation of PC's railroad assets. As part of the legislation that authorized the creation of Conrail, Amtrak assumed operation of former Penn Central coach yards, maintenance facilities, and shops at many strategic locations, including Boston, New Haven, Wilmington (Delaware), Philadelphia, Ivy City (Washington, D.C.), and Chicago. These facilities put Amtrak in a much better position to service, maintain, and repair its own equipment and to earn money by providing contract work to suburban passenger carriers and others.

More controversial was Amtrak's acquisition of several major routes, most notably the

In April 1987, Amtrak discontinued the *Montrealer* because it claimed the tracks maintained by Boston & Maine were too poor to continue service. Congress had granted Amtrak condemnation power over freight railroads in order to maintain service, and Amtrak was forced to exercise this power to restore the *Montrealer*. Amtrak acquired B&M's Connecticut River Line and sold it to the Central Vermont Railway, but B&M's owners fought the decision. The case went all the way to the U.S. Supreme Court, which ruled in Amtrak's favor. On July 17, 1989, Amtrak ran a special train on the Central Vermont inaugurating the renewed *Montrealer*. *Brian Solomon*

Boston–New York City–Washington, D.C., Northeast Corridor. This largely passenger route had benefited from considerable federal investment over the previous five decades. In early 1976, President Gerald Ford signed legislation authorizing $1.6 billion for NEC improvements. In addition, Amtrak was given authority to acquire the NEC Penn Central route. However, the Department of Transportation, under Secretary William T. Coleman, argued against the transfer of the NEC to Amtrak on grounds that it was not in public interest. Amtrak, under Reistrup's direction, paid $87 million to Conrail, a price set by the United States Railway Association (the agency that oversaw the planning and creation of Conrail, not to be confused with the World War I–era United States Railway Administration), in order to take title of NEC on April 1, 1976, the day that Conrail began operations.

Outraged, Secretary Coleman withheld Amtrak's operating subsidy in protest, leading to congressional hearings in the summer of 1976. In defense of his actions, Coleman's explained in his August 10, 1976, testimony to Congress, "Once Amtrak owns the corridor properties, the federal government will lose the capacity to insure that the project is implemented effectively, because, as owner, Amtrak can refuse access to its property to any party and on any basis that it sees fit, unless there is prior agreement to the contrary."

One of the smallest communities served by Amtrak was the isolated town of Thompson, Utah, along the old Denver & Rio Grande Western, which was a flag stop on the *California Zephyr*. Amtrak has since moved the flag stop west to Green River, Utah. *Brian Solomon*

Congress sided with Reistrup, and Amtrak's ownership of the Northeast Corridor was secured. Improvements began on March 31, 1977. The plan was to rehabilitate tracks, electrification, and signaling systems, plus electrify the gap between New Haven, Connecticut, and Boston to allow for greatly improved running times. It was hoped that by 1981 trains would run on 3-hour-40-minute schedules between Boston and New York's Penn Station and on 2-hour-40-minute schedules between Penn Station and Washington, D.C.

Rain on Amtrak's Parade

Like dark clouds on a summer day, events in 1977 foreshadowed an end to Amtrak's rosy vision of the future. Its ridership exceeded 19 million yearly passengers, and it forecasted carrying 26 million annual passengers by 1982.

Overall, service had improved dramatically since 1971, and Amtrak had bold plans for further improvement. It was rebuilding the NEC and planning to buy hundreds of additional new cars and modernize its maintenance facilities. Reistrup sought funding increases to improve key freight lines that Amtrak utilized to allow for higher speeds.

The year didn't start out well. In January unusually bad weather made a mockery of Amtrak's schedules and revealed the worst characteristics of steam-heated passenger equipment. But it wasn't just the inherited equipment that was causing problems. Amtrak's flawed E60 electrics had already made the news. Also in January, Amtrak's relatively new fleet of SDP40F diesels was suspected of causing a number of derailments, some serious, which resulted in tough speed restrictions (see Chapter 3). Although relief was on the way as the last of Amtrak's new Amfleet cars were delivered, Congress and the newly elected Carter administration voiced concerns over Amtrak's relative performance and perceived high costs.

Yet, Amtrak's woes were only part of a bigger and much gloomier picture for railroads. The recently formed Conrail system hadn't cured the problems of the bankrupt freight carriers whose operations it had assumed. Despite considerable influx of federal funds, Conrail wasn't showing any signs of becoming profitable. Worse, the industry as a whole appeared to be weakening.

By the fall of 1977, Amtrak was reaching a funding shortfall. When Reistrup asked Congress for additional money to cover its operating deficit, he was rebuffed and the money denied. To save money, Amtrak implemented nominal cuts on the NEC and threatened deeper cuts if money wasn't found. As reported in the October 12, 1977, *Washington Post*, Reistrup explained to Congress that if America desired passenger service, "then its funding level should permit such a system to be developed and operated properly." Reistrup added that if not, then "maybe we should eliminate it entirely."

In just a few months Amtrak went from anticipating expansion to fending off oblivion. Congress and the Carter administration made it clear that they felt Amtrak was costing too much and needed to be scaled back. Some in Congress took a more extreme outlook and suggested placing Amtrak under direct government control. In early 1978, plans were being discussed to eliminate Amtrak's least viable routes. President Jimmy Carter's secretary of transportation, Brock Adams, made it clear that it wasn't a matter of whether Amtrak should be pruned, but rather, which lines should be cut. Reistrup, who had helped resurrect American passenger service and brought it to its highest level of service in decades and who had bright visions for the

Chicago architect Daniel H. Burnham designed Washington Union Station in the Beaux Arts style, which incorporated classical motifs and materials. The station was opened in 1907 and completed in 1908. Sadly, the building was allowed to deteriorate so badly that by 1981 it was deemed a safety hazard and closed. It was nearly demolished, but instead Amtrak gave it a multimillion-dollar renovation and it reopened in September 1988. Today, it is one of the most beautiful buildings served by Amtrak. *Brian Solomon*

future, was dismayed and frustrated by the political climate and resigned Amtrak's presidency in June 1978. Don Phillips, writing as "The Potomac Pundit" in the July 1978 *TRAINS* magazine, stated, "For 3 years 3 months, [Reistrup] lived in a world that made little sense, a world in which he was told by Congress and the current administration to run a quality passenger service but not to expect enough money to do the job." Phillips quoted Reistrup's far-sighted prediction that Amtrak was in for "a period of turmoil that will be

Many of Amtrak's passenger stops are the traditional stations once used by the private railroads. One classic is the old Atlantic Coast Line (later Seaboard Coast Line) Spanish Revival-style station in Orlando, Florida, designed by M. A. Griffith and completed in 1927. Where this station once hosted ACL's *West Coast Champion* and *Havana Special*, today it serves Amtrak's *Silver Star*, *Silver Meteor*, and the tri-weekly *Sunset Limited*. Brian Solomon

very severe, like a cold front coming through." For his part, Reistrup explained—with no regrets—that he had failed to coordinate intercity buses and passenger trains and that he hadn't moved fast enough to adopt the F40PH type of locomotive and to convert conventional steam-heated equipment to Head End Power (HEP), in which a centrally located source provides all of a train's non-tractive and non-motive power needs. He also wished he had taken "personal control over the Northeast Corridor sooner."

A New, Slimmer Amtrak

Alan Boyd assumed Amtrak's presidency in the summer of 1978. Like Reistrup, Boyd came from the management of Illinois Central, but he was most familiar to the railroad industry as the first Secretary of Transportation. He recognized Amtrak's political predicament and

worked with Congress and Adams to scale back operations. Boyd told Congress "Amtrak—as a public service—is plainly spread too thin."

David P. Morgan, in the July 1980 *TRAINS*, quoted Boyd: "One train a day anywhere can be little more than a costly curiosity, like the circus which comes to town each year."

Morgan elaborated on Boyd's philosophy, explaining that Boyd believed Amtrak's future was in the development of corridor services and that all Amtrak stations should have daylight services. There was little question of Amtrak's continued need for subsidy and for the validity of the service it provided.

Ironically, on February 1, 1979, with studies under way to determine which services to cut, Amtrak assumed operation of the Southern Railway's *Crescent*. Under the administration of W. Graham Claytor Jr.,

the Southern Railway had remained out of Amtrak, operating its own passenger trains at a multimillion-dollar loss. Many believed the *Crescent* was the finest train left in America. When Claytor retired, his successor, cost-conscious L. Stanley Crane, chose to join Amtrak and end the Southern's stockholder subsidy of the *Crescent*. Although Amtrak assumed operation of the *Crescent*, the train was not exempted from consideration for elimination, although in the end, Amtrak retained the popular route.

In the autumn of 1979, Adams drafted a list of cuts, hoping to trim Amtrak's route structure from 27,500 miles to just 15,700. The weakest-performing trains were to be eliminated to allow Amtrak to refocus resources on better-performing runs. Although less severe than Adams had intended, in October 1979 Amtrak implemented the most radical service changes since its inception. Among the trains cut was the Washington, D.C.–Catlettsburg, Kentucky, *Hilltopper*, which had suffered the repeated ignominy of being cited by critics as an example of everything that was wrong with Amtrak. Also sacked were the Chicago– Miami *Floridian*, the New York City–Pittsburgh–Kansas City *National Limited*, the New York–Florida *Champion*, the Chicago–Seattle *North Coast Hiawatha*, and the Chicago–Texas *Lone Star*. In addition, there were a few routing adjustments.

At this time, Amtrak also introduced new routes and improved services. The *Desert Wind* began operation over Union Pacific trackage between Ogden, Utah, and Los Angeles. The *Lake Shore Limited* saw a twofold upgrade: the introduction of refurbished HEP-equipped heritage cars and the reopening of 12 miles of the old Boston & Albany between Post Road and Rensselaer, New York (abandoned by PC

The old Santa Fe depot at Raton, New Mexico, serves Amtrak's daily *Southwest Chief*. This Mission-style station was completed by Santa Fe in 1904 and once housed a Fred Harvey restaurant. In its day, the Fred Harvey chain provided a higher class of meal service for Santa Fe passengers than was available on most American railroads. Fred Harvey was associated with quality, service, and his attractive young waitresses, known as Harvey Girls. *Brian Solomon*

A pair of brand-new GENESIS diesels leads the *Southwest Chief* downgrade on the Santa Fe toward Pica, Arizona. Up front, ahead of the passenger-carrying Superliners, are material-handling cars (MHCs) used to transport mail and express. During the Claytor era, Amtrak bought a fleet of MHCs equipped with high-speed trucks to operate as fast as passenger cars. Santa Fe was equipped with automatic train stop that permitted a top speed of 90 miles per hour for passenger trains. *Brian Solomon*

in 1973) to tighten schedules on the Boston section. Amtrak's long-awaited Superliners were assigned first to the *Empire Builder*.

Amtrak Fights for Survival

The 1980s brought tough times for Amtrak.

Where President Carter had demanded a slimmer Amtrak, the new Reagan administration wanted to slash its federal subsidy and ultimately eliminate it entirely. Reistrup's prediction of severe turmoil proved true. Throughout the 1980s, Amtrak waged a highly publicized fight to retain its subsidy.

At the end of September 1981, Amtrak implemented another round of service cuts as a result of budget tightening. Among the casualties were the *Black Hawk* and *Pacific International*. The *Shenandoah* was replaced by the restored *Capitol Limited*, providing direct

Chicago–Pittsburgh–Washington, D.C., service over the old B&O route.

NEC electrification, torpedoing the age-old dream of high-speed electric service between New York City and Boston. Don Phillips quoted Reagan's budget director David Stockman in the May 1981 issue of *TRAINS* as explaining that the Northeast Corridor Improvement Project "places needless emphasis on improving trip time."

Ironically, the Reagan administration gave Amtrak one of its most dynamic leaders. According to Wilner, Reagan's transportation secretary, Drew Lewis, greatly admired former Southern Railway President Claytor and promoted him as the best man to run Amtrak. Claytor was a well-respected railroader and had been vocal in his criticism of Amtrak in its early years. He had also demonstrated what a private company could do with passenger service. On July 2, 1982, Claytor became Amtrak's fourth president despite the fact he was a Democrat in a Republican administration.

Although Amtrak faced a cloudy political climate, when Claytor took the throttle the railroad was in the best shape physically since

Continued on page 56

Amtrak employees prepare to unload material-handling cars at New Haven, Connecticut. *Brian Solomon*

Gil Reid:
Master Calendar Artist

By John Gruber

Gil Reid, who produced 18 calendar paintings from 1974 to 1992, plus an unpublished view of the *Sunset Limited* and two earlier paintings for Auto-Liner, which also were used by Amtrak, remains the king of Amtrak artists.

Today, Reid's paintings hang in Amtrak offices in Washington, D.C., where David L. Gunn, in one of his first moves as president, restored the watercolors to a place of honor. When looking over his new offices on a Saturday, Gunn found the paintings stored in a closet. He went to a hardware store, purchased hangers, and put the paintings on the walls for all the employees to see when they arrived at work the next Monday.

No one has even come close to Reid's record at Amtrak. J. Craig Thorpe painted calendars for 1993, 1995, and 1996. Ted Rose also did three, for 1997, 1998, and 1999. Bill Kratville initiated the Auto-Liner calendars shared with Amtrak for 1971 and 1972.

Bruce Heard, who retired in 2001, worked with Reid for 19 years. While in the Government and Public Affairs Department, Heard was responsible for the development and production of Amtrak's calendar series, including checking press proofs at the printer. When W. Graham Claytor Jr. was Amtrak's president, the subject of the painting usually was a closely guarded secret, shared only by Claytor, Heard, and Reid until the calendar was distributed.

Reid recalled how the calendars were approved. "Heard would take a painting that I had done to Claytor, and he and Graham would say, 'Fine, what do we do next year?' If Graham didn't [ask] that, Bruce would say, 'Gil's got an idea for next year's calendar.' 'OK, what is it? Tell him to print it.' It was all done on a handshake, with no contract or anything like that."

Heard continued, "Initially I merely provided suggestions to the Amtrak public affairs people who worked directly with Gil on Amtrak's behalf. By 1982, I had become totally responsible for the calendar project and I continued in that position, overseeing Gil's work on a total of 11 pieces of art for the calendar."

GIL REID 1991

For 1994, Gil created a spectacular painting that commemorated the *Sunset Limited* as Amtrak's first transcontinental train. The scene depicted a steam-powered 1928-vintage *Sunset Limited* complete with open-platform observation car and drumhead, along with Amtrak's contemporary Superliner-equipped *Sunset Limited*. But this 1994 calendar was not meant to be. On September 22, 1993, a barge knocked a bridge out of alignment near Mobile,

Amtrak's 1992 calendar featured this painting by Gil Reid depicting three generations of the *Crescent*. Amtrak had assumed operation of the *Crescent* from the Southern Railway in 1979. The New York City-Washington, D.C.-New Orleans *Crescent* was Amtrak's 1992 train of the year. *Painting by Gil Reid, courtesy of Amtrak*

Alabama, and when the *Sunset Limited* subsequently traversed over the bridge, many of the cars on the train sank. Five crewmembers and 42 passengers lost their lives in the worst wreck in Amtrak history. As a result, Gil's painting was not used for the 1994 calendar, and Marty Katz made a hastily set up photograph of the X2000 Swedish tilt train, the German Intercity City Express (ICE train, and an Amtrak AMD-103 locomotive.

Reid, who worked for Kalmbach Publishing Company for 21 years, maintained a studio with a view of the ex-Milwaukee Road mainline in Elm Grove, Wisconsin, until 2003. At age 86, he now paints from his home, recounting clay tennis courts and encounters with junkyard dogs and sharing other memories of the Amtrak series.

its birth. Despite curtailed electrification plans, the NEC had been largely rebuilt with concrete ties and welded rails. Amtrak's passenger fleet now consisted of hundreds of new Amfleet and Superliner cars, with additional Amfleet II cars under construction. Many of its older cars had been rebuilt with HEP as the Heritage Fleet, and the majority of steam-heated cars had been retired. Amtrak had a nearly new fleet of F40PH diesels and AEM-7 electrics. In 1972, 22 years was the average age of both Amtrak passenger cars and locomotives. By 1982, the average age of cars was 14 years, while the average age of passenger service locomotives was just four years.

Word Wars

Claytor fought an ideological battle with the Reagan administration. Budget director Stockman despised Amtrak. Wilner notes that in his 1985 State of the Union speech, Ronald Reagan lambasted Amtrak's wastefulness, saying

he last westward *Black Hawk* at Freeport, Illinois, on September 30, 1981, one of several victims of Reagan-era budget cuts. Partly funded by Illinois, the *Black Hawk* began operation in 1974, using the Illinois Central Gulf route connecting Chicago and Dubuque, Iowa. Its discontinuance left Illinois' second largest city, Rockford, without rail passenger service. *John Gruber*

"taxpayers pay about $35 per passenger every time an Amtrak train leaves the station [and] it's time we ended this huge lower-case federal subsidy."

Claytor fired back that the federal government subsidized "each major airline passenger to the tune of $42." He also pointed out in a November 15, 1985, letter to the *New York Times* that "of total Federal spending, Amtrak exacts a tiny seven hundredths of 1 percent."

One of the busiest mountain mainlines in the United States is the Union Pacific freight route between Granger, Wyoming, and Portland, Oregon. Today, this route accommodates approximately 50 million tons of freight annually. Until 1997, Amtrak's *Pioneer* traversed most of this route. On June 12, 1993, Amtrak No. 25, the westward *Pioneer*, negotiates the Leonard Horseshoe near Durkee, Oregon, on its ascent of Encina Hill. *Brian Solomon*

Public criticism of Amtrak, however, only had the effect of rallying support both in Washington and in the cities and towns along its lines. Amtrak had friends in high places,

State-sponsored corridors allow Amtrak to operate intensive regional services above and beyond its basic network. California's Capitol Corridor is a model for success. In a 1990 ballot, California voters approved bond issues largely drafted by the Train Riders Association of California to fund rail expansion. Services began in late 1991 and have enjoyed enormous growth. A San Jose–bound *Capitol* hugs the shore of San Pablo Bay in August 1993. *Brian Solomon*

especially Congress. Every year, the Reagan administration zeroed Amtrak's funding, and every year Congress restored it. While Amtrak made lots of negative headlines, it survived from year to year. If its supporters had backed off at any time, Amtrak may have gone the way of the trolley car.

Return of the Zephyr

Unlike the 1970s when Amtrak saw numerous changes in route structure, during the Reagan years its map remained fairly constant; however, there were some significant adjustments. In 1983, Rio Grande finally joined Amtrak, permitting Amtrak to route its Chicago–Oakland service over Rio Grande's scenic crossing of the Rockies and adopt the name *California Zephyr*, which had been one of America's best-known streamliners. Amtrak's *California Zephyr* traces most of the route of the original train between Chicago and

some $6 million annually to help reduce subsidies needed for other Amtrak trains."

Other 1980s additions to the Amtrak network included Atlantic City services and seasonal weekend *Cape Codder* trains, both of which were relatively short-lived.

Labor Reform

Continued budget threats forced Amtrak to cut its labor costs. In 1982, Amtrak led the way in railroad labor reform, negotiating progressive work rules with its unions to enhance employee productivity. Unions agreed to abolish traditional crew districts that dated back to the steam era. Traditionally, passenger crew districts were just 100 to 150 miles long, and typically a crew would earn a full day's pay running the length of the district, even if this was accomplished in just a few hours. Under the new rules, crews were paid based on an eight-hour day and might run several hundred miles a day to earn their pay. In January 1983, Amtrak began using its own operating crews on the NEC and over the next few years began using its own operating crews systemwide. By 1988, virtually all train crews on Amtrak trains were Amtrak employees.

Amtrak Diversifies

Amtrak's charter included provisions to handle mail and express traffic. During the 1980s, Amtrak greatly expanded its mail and express capacity. According to Mike Schafer's *All Aboard Amtrak*, in 1984 Amtrak reintroduced dedicated mail trains along the NEC. Between 1986 and 1988, Amtrak purchased a fleet of 160 specially designed material handling cars (MHCs) from Thrall. These cars, along with Heritage Fleet baggage cars, became a common sight on most Amtrak long-distance trains. In some situations, the large number of MHCs at the front of passenger trains made them appear like the old mixed trains that carried both freight and passenger cars.

When Amtrak was created it was prohibited from running commuter rail operations. Initially,

Winnemucca, Nevada; from that point it traverses the former Southern Pacific's route over Donner Pass, a scenic line in its own right.

October 1983 saw the inauguration of Amtrak's *Auto Train* service between Lorton, Virginia, and Sanford, Florida. Despite the bankruptcy of the original Auto-Train, which operated between 1972 and 1981, in the last 20 years Amtrak has developed this car-ferry as one of its most successful services. Wilner notes that by 1993 Amtrak's *Auto Train* was "one of its few long-distance trains that recovers more than its long-term costs, contributing these services were retained by the private railroads. Gradually, over the next decade, state and local commuter rail agencies and operational authorities were established to subsidize and run suburban commuter trains. Legislation was changed, and in the early 1980s Amtrak anticipated the need for contract commuter operators and entered the business of providing contract-rail operations to commuter agencies. By the early 1990s, Amtrak was carrying more annual passengers on its contract commuter trains than on its long-distance trains.

Its first contract operation was with the Maryland Department of Transportation to operate Baltimore–Washington, D.C., trains over the NEC. In 1987, Amtrak secured its first large-scale commuter contract with the Massachusetts Bay Transportation Authority (MBTA). According to the April 1987 *CTC Board*, at that time MBTA was running more than 270 trains daily on nine routes. Amtrak operated Boston suburban services from 1987 until 2003. In 1990, Amtrak took on Connecticut's Shore Line East commuter services between New Haven and, initially, Old Saybrook, Connecticut. By the mid-1990s, Amtrak was also operating Virginia Railway Express in the Washington, D.C., suburbs, MetroLink in Los Angeles, San Diego–Oceanside, California, *Coaster* services,

and the former Southern Pacific San Francisco–San Jose Peninsula "commutes."

Healthier Amtrak

Increased labor productivity and greater revenue through mail and express business and commuter rail contracts plus a steady climb in rail passengers enabled Amtrak to greatly improve its revenue-to-cost ratio in the Claytor period. Phillips, writing in the *Washington Post* on December 1, 1993, explained that in 1982 Amtrak revenue covered only 53 percent of its operating costs. Ten years later its revenue covered 79 percent of its operating costs. As a result, it needed substantially less federal operating subsidies in the early 1990s.

Claytor remained the head of Amtrak for more than a decade, retiring in 1993 after it seemed that Amtrak's future was assured with Bill Clinton as president. Claytor was 81 upon his retirement, making him the oldest and the longest-serving Amtrak president. Sadly, he died only six months after retirement. He is remembered fondly by those who knew and worked with him and is widely credited for saving Amtrak during one of its most trying times.

Amtrak's *Acela Express* connects Boston and Washington, D.C., using custom-designed high-speed tilting trains. Tilting cars reduce the unpleasant effects of centrifugal forces on passengers, allowing for fast operation in curves. A Washington-Boston *Acela Express* negotiates the reverse curve at Elizabeth, New Jersey. *Patrick Yough*

CHAPTER TWO

AMTRAK IN MODERN TIMES

Industry Transformation

Decades of weak financial performance and the specter of financial collapse finally resulted in government deregulation of the American railroad industry during the late 1970s. This culminated with the Staggers Act of 1980. Rate deregulation removed the chains that had stifled the freight railroads for years, encouraging them to implement innovative practices and technology that transformed the industry during the 1980s.

The *Hoosier State* at sunset, March 18, 1995, has just passed South Raub, Indiana. This train was one of several runs cut during 1995 budget tightening. *Pete Ruesch*

By the late 1980s, the railroads were hauling record amounts of freight using fewer mainlines, fewer employers, and fewer locomotives, while earning decent profits. Fears of financial doom and the prospects of nationalization had abated. During this time there was renewed merger activity: Norfolk & Western merged with Southern; CSX was formed, combining the Chessie System, Louisville & Nashville, Seaboard Coast Line, and others; Union Pacific absorbed Missouri Pacific, Western Pacific, and later the Missouri–Kansas–Texas.

Changes in freight railroading had a variety of implications for Amtrak. As a result of the traffic boom, many of the freight lines that hosted Amtrak trains were much busier, while consolidation resulted in other lines being downgraded and some abandoned. Freight railroads were enjoying heavier traffic, but management that had spent four decades consistently downsizing physical plant was hesitant to spend money to add capacity on the remaining lines. In a speech to the Western Railway Club of Chicago on March 20, 1989, Amtrak President W. Graham Claytor said:

Not too long ago, when the freight business was a little slack, several of our freight railroad partners were urging us to add more passenger service on their lines for this reason. . . . I find somewhat less enthusiasm about Amtrak when freight traffic is up, as it is today, but I hope to be looked on as a partner and good customer in good times as well as bad.

Traffic continued to rise through the 1990s. While some railroads have invested in additional capacity—installing more mainline tracks, lengthening passing sidings, and improving signaling—railroad congestion has become a serious problem. Because passenger trains have inherently different infrastructure requirements than freight—they are shorter, faster, and lighter and need to adhere to tighter

GENESIS P42s 11 and 30 lead Amtrak No. 40, the *Three Rivers*, east along the former Pennsylvania Railroad Middle Division near Union Furnace, Pennsylvania, in November 1998. In 1995, Amtrak replaced its New York City-Chicago *Broadway Limited* with the New York City-Pittsburgh *Three Rivers*. Within a few years the *Three Rivers* was extended to Chicago. Both trains used the same road numbers, 40 and 41. *Brian Solomon*

On September 27, 1997, the *Capitol Limited* makes its station stop at Cumberland, Maryland. This train will resume its eastward journey and follow the Potomac River toward Washington, D.C. Today, the *Capitol Limited* is one of a few eastern trains that use Superliner bi-levels. *Brian Solomon*

schedules—they place different and often conflicting requirements on railroad operations. The particulars of American freight operations are too complex for the scope of this text, but suffice it to say, freight trains typically run long and heavy, do not need tight schedules for intermediate stops between terminals, and sometimes run with schedules designated by days rather than minutes. As freight train lengths increase more problems can develop when the train is on the road. A delay of an hour means little to the customer of a coal train, but makes a big difference to the customer of an Amtrak train following on the same track.

Amtrak is a freight railroad customer, but a very high-maintenance customer—literally and figuratively—whose requirements sometimes conflict with those of its hosts. The results are delayed trains, rough-riding track, and freight railroad management opposing expanded passenger schedules. Some freight lines view Amtrak as a poor use of track space. In their eyes high-value freight traffic is easier to handle and more lucrative than Amtrak's passenger trains.

Not every situation results in confrontation or opposition. During the 1990s, some railroads recognized that Amtrak and commuter railroads could help them solve congestion problems. In some situations, the desire for Amtrak services has provided freight railroads with capital to repair and rebuild their lines to increase speeds and capacity. This benefits both Amtrak and the freight railroads.

In 1996, 25 years after it was formed, Amtrak needed to renew and renegotiate its contracts. In 1971, the railroads were eager to get rid of their passenger trains and were relieved that Amtrak would assume their financial burden. By 1996, railroads' outlooks had changed, giving Amtrak less leverage to negotiate. As a result, Amtrak had to pay more or receive less.

Renewing an Amtrak Myth

One of Claytor's crusades was to secure long-term funding through a one-cent gasoline tax (the "Ampenny"). In the December 1991 issue of *Railway Gazette International*, Claytor wrote that Amtrak was "on a clear track toward full-recovery of [its] operating costs from revenue." This philosophy renewed the self-sufficiency concept, which Claytor said could be achieved if Amtrak services could be continually improved to meet demand, and its services could be expanded to increase its revenue base. Most important, Claytor added, Amtrak needed sufficient capital to achieve these goals. Claytor's optimism was based on Amtrak's progress during the 1980s, when it improved both productivity and ridership while reducing dependency on federal subsidy. Claytor hoped to increase revenue by expanding passenger service as well as other businesses, especially its mail and express service and its contract commuter business.

Unfortunately, Claytor's vision renewed the myth that Amtrak *would* become self-sustaining and even profitable—the imperative message that Amtrak required significant capital investment to continually improve and expand service was largely forgotten. Worse, Claytor's

In September 1998, the *Southwest Chief* races east of Las Vegas, New Mexico, passing old Santa Fe upper-quadrant semaphores. Santa Fe and its successor, Burlington Northern Santa Fe, route most freight traffic via the more-southern transcontinental route that uses the Belen cutoff. This leaves the northerly route free of most freight traffic and open for fast passenger running. The downside is that BNSF would like to sell its northerly line. *Brian Solomon*

Clearing milepost 103 on the Union Pacific's Glidden Subdivision, the *Sunset Limited* rolls eastward at sunset near Schulenburg, Texas, on December 14, 2002. At 2,764 miles, the *Sunset Limited* is Amtrak's longest run, connecting Orlando with Los Angeles. It takes the better part of three days to cover this distance while passing through the varied scenery of farmland, swamps, thick forests, and high desert mountains. *Tom Kline*

hopes of securing the Ampenny faded and the yearly begging routine continued.

In the early 1990s, Amtrak did make nominal investment in new equipment, financing the construction of GENESIS locomotives and Superliner II and Viewliner passenger cars, all of which were needed to replace aging equipment and to maintain service. However, Amtrak did not substantially improve or expand its level of service. For example, the order for Viewliners, which was originally supposed to include a variety of car types, in the end was limited to just sleeping cars.

Renewed Northeast Corridor Improvement

One area where Amtrak made progress was with Northeast Corridor (NEC) improvements. In 1991, Congress appropriated some money for capital improvements, which renewed the effort to revitalize and improve Amtrak's busiest route. Amtrak imported high-speed streamlined trains from Europe for testing on the NEC; in 1992, a Swedish X2000 train arrived, followed by a German Intercity City Express (ICE) train-set in 1993. In addition to NEC testing, both trains made national tours, towed by diesel locomotives, to help generate interest in high-speed rail. The Federal Railway Administration officially recommended electrifying from Boston to New Haven, Connecticut, over the Shoreline route in 1994. This ultimately led to the financing

of infrastructure improvements and the development and purchase of high-speed trains for Boston–New York–Washington, D.C., service.

On July 3, 1996, Amtrak hosted a groundbreaking ceremony in Providence, Rhode Island, symbolic because it was where Senator Claiborne Pell had first conceived the idea of high-speed service on the NEC in the early 1960s. Pell, on the eve of his retirement from the Senate, was among the guests.

Funding Crisis . . . 1990s Style

During the early 1990s, despite talk of capital improvements and experiments with European trains, Amtrak quietly suffered from neglect of its basic hardware. During the 1992 presidential campaign, Democratic candidates Bill Clinton and Al Gore had voiced support for rail travel, declaring their desire to make Amtrak a "world-class passenger railroad." Once elected, however, they didn't deliver substantive capital investment. Amtrak's needs were forgotten when more pressing issues regarding the national budget deficit took political precedence. The Clinton administration did not publicly try to kill Amtrak funding, as was the case during the Reagan years, but neither did it give Amtrak the capital it needed. Although it seemed that the threat to Amtrak had subsided, in reality it just took a new form. Many Amtrak supporters mistakenly believed that Amtrak's future was secure. In fact, it was in jeopardy.

Thomas M. Downs assumed Amtrak's presidency in December 1993 following Claytor's retirement. However, by early 1994 it was becoming clear that Amtrak was in financial trouble. But its problems lay largely

The eastbound *Cardinal* stops for passengers at Lafayette, Indiana, in February 1996. In addition to providing an additional route between East Coast cities and Chicago, the *Cardinal* serves many communities in rural Appalachia and the Midwest, including Indianapolis. *Pete Ruesch*

Amtrak provides bus connections allowing passengers to reach more destinations. This Amtrak California decal was photographed at Colfax, California, on the side of a bus that provides service to passengers and commuters in towns of the Sacramento valley foothills. *Tom Kline*

outside the NEC, which had finally received needed investment.

On March 18, 1994, Don Phillips reported in the *Washington Post* on the seriousness of Amtrak's condition. Kenneth M. Mead, director of transportation for the general accounting office, explained that for many years, Amtrak had made up shortfalls in its operating budget by diverting funds intended to buy new equipment and maintenance. The effects of the starvation budget during the Reagan years were finally catching up. Unfortunately, now Amtrak was facing a multifaceted crisis. In addition to immediate funding, Amtrak's 25-year contracts with freight railroads, signed in 1971, were due to expire, and it needed to negotiate new labor agreements with 14 of its unions between 1994 and 1997.

By the end of 1994, a serious cash crunch forced Amtrak to take drastic action. In a repeat of the late-1970s crisis, Amtrak curtailed services, cutting both trains and routes, and implemented significant labor cuts. At that time, Amtrak was carrying 22 million passengers annually (excluding contract commuter operations). According to *Passenger Train Journal* (*PTJ*), it planned to trim services by 21 percent. Amtrak hired consultants to help decide which trains to cut. Part of Amtrak's strategy

was to encourage the states to increase subsidies for regional services.

Unlike the 1979 decimation of services, Amtrak implemented these cuts in phases. In February 1995 it cut the *Palmetto* and reduced service levels on the *Empire Builder, Crescent,* and *Desert Wind* from daily to roughly every other day. April 1995 cuts were more severe.

Amtrak reduced the levels of service on the Chicago–Milwaukee Hiawatha Corridor; the Chicago–Detroit Corridor; New York's Empire Corridor; and the Boston–Springfield, Massachusetts–New Haven Inland Corridor. Service to Atlantic City, New Jersey, was eliminated (although NJ Transit local operations remained), as was the New Orleans–Mobile,

Amtrak's *Keystone* services between Philadelphia and Harrisburg are funded in part by the Pennsylvania DOT. These trains use the former Pennsylvania Railroad Main Line. Although the route is electrified, Amtrak trains have been typically diesel-hauled in recent years. *Keystone* No. 646 passes Overbrook, Pennsylvania, on its way to 30th Street Station in Philadelphia on February 25, 2004. *Brian Solomon*

Continued on page 74

The Raleigh-Charlotte *Piedmont* approaches its station stop at Durham, North Carolina, on February 19, 2004. This three-car train is hauled by F59PHI 1755 *City of Salisbury.* North Carolina DOT's Ellen Holding designed the locomotive's livery, an adaptation of the state flag. North Carolina DOT specifically selected heritage passenger equipment for the *Piedmont* because of lower long-term costs. *Brian Solomon*

Amtrak in North Carolina

In the wake of insufficient federal funding, much of Amtrak's growth outside the Boston–Washington, D.C., Northeast Corridor has been state-sponsored. California, Illinois, Maine, Massachusetts, New York, and Washington are among the states that have demonstrated what can be accomplished with local financing and planning. Medium-distance corridors, typically defined as involving trips of less than 500 miles, have some of the strongest growth potential for Amtrak. To serve these corridors effectively, multiple roundtrips on competitive schedules are necessary.

Developing an effective corridor requires cooperation between state and federal authorities and between Amtrak and privately operated freight railroads,

which own the majority of railroad infrastructure in the United States and typically only maintain it at levels required for their freight operations. The development of passenger corridors requires infrastructure investment to allow for more trains and higher running speeds.

North Carolina has been one of the most progressive states in developing and planning passenger rail expansion and improvement. This has been driven by North Carolinian's passion for passenger trains and a growing need for alternatives to highway and air transport. In 1984 and 1985 the state funded the experimental *Carolinian* service between Charlotte, North Carolina, and New York City. In 1990, this service was reintroduced as a permanent run, with North

In 1995, North Carolina inaugurated its first modern intrastate service with the Raleigh-Charlotte *Piedmont*. This service uses equipment owned by North Carolina DOT and operated under contract by Amtrak, similar to the California corridor services. Initially the *Piedmont* was hauled with GP40PH-2s, locomotives remanufactured from EMD GP40s. Passenger equipment consisted of former Kansas City Southern coaches refurbished by the Delaware Car Company of Wilmington, Delaware. In addition, a former Milwaukee Road full-length dome was used for a few years as a lounge. In 1998, North Carolina DOT bought two new EMD F59PHI locomotives for the *Piedmont*.

North Carolina DOT has reinforced its commitment to passenger services by investing $110 million in station rehabilitation and station construction using a mix of federal, state, and local funding. In addition, it has worked with Norfolk Southern to improve track speed and capacity. Recently the single-track Cary-Greensboro section of the NCR was improved, with its sidings lengthened and centralized traffic control signaling installed to better integrate freight and passenger services and increase track speed. In addition, in mid-2004, four quadrant grade-crossing gates were being installed at key road crossings. Such improvements have shaved 20-30 minutes off the *Piedmont*'s schedule, and in 2002, statewide Amtrak trains were carrying 442,000 passengers annually.

North Carolina has ambitious plans for future passenger rail development, including the restoration of service over the old Southern between Salisbury and Asheville. North Carolina is on the Federal Railroad Administration's Southeast High-Speed Rail Corridor, and to date has made the most investment of the four states on this planned route. Eventually, North Carolina would like to boost top speeds to 110 miles per hour on portions of this route, and has recognized that rail development is a more cost-effective transport solution than continued highway development. By working with Norfolk Southern and CSX to improve its rail infrastructure, North Carolina hopes to provide time-competitive rail service to its largest urban areas and to move 1.6 million passengers annually by 2015. This proactive approach toward passenger rail development is an excellent example of what can be accomplished on a state level.

Carolina covering the expense of running the train south of Richmond, Virginia. Today, based on cost recovery, it is one of the most successful trains on Amtrak.

In the 1990s, North Carolina began planning the development of intrastate passenger services. North Carolina has historically actively developed railroads. In fact, former Governor John Motley Morehead led the charge for the state to finance and build a railroad in the mid-1800s to connect some of the state's major cities. The state now holds 100 percent of the shares of the North Carolina Railroad (NCR), which leases its lines to Norfolk Southern. In the late 1990s, North Carolina bought the remaining private shares of the company in order to give it a better bargaining position with Norfolk Southern to improve railroad infrastructure for passenger train expansion.

Alabama, *Gulf Breeze*. The overnight Washington, D.C.–New York City–Montreal *Montrealer* was cancelled and replaced with a Vermont-sponsored day train to St. Albans called the *Vermonter*. In the summer of 1995 Amtrak killed additional long-distance passenger trains, including its famous New York City–Chicago *Broadway Limited*, one of the few remaining name trains that Amtrak had inherited from its predecessors. Some of the services curtailed during this period were restored, as states came up with additional funding.

Eliminating long-distance services that relied on heritage equipment had another benefit: it allowed Amtrak to retire passenger cars that would have needed the addition of chemical retention toilets in order to comply with new regulations.

According to *Passenger Train Journal*, labor reductions trimmed an estimated 36 percent of management jobs, resulting in nearly 600 people leaving Amtrak and a 24 percent cut in union labor. The short-term benefit of reduced labor helped Amtrak make up its cash shortfall, but had the negative effect of a skills drain. Many of Amtrak's most experienced people left, some of whom had worked for the company for the better part of two decades.

Running Amtrak Like a Business

Tom Downs' strategy for Amtrak embraced the Claytor-inspired theory of attaining self-sufficiency through the growth of Amtrak's freight businesses and running Amtrak like a modern business. Elimination of one-third of management was a step toward Downs' larger reorganization in which he divided Amtrak into three regional business units: Northeast Corridor, Western, and Intercity. The Northeast Corridor unit consisted of most northeastern regional services, including the Empire Corridor, Keystone services, and New York City–Montreal service. The Western unit, known as Amtrak West, consisted of services in California, Oregon, and Washington State,

including California's *San Diegan*s—known as *Pacific Surfliner*s after June 2000—(San Diego–Los Angeles–San Luis Obispo), *San Joaquin*s (Oakland–Bakersfield), and *Capitol*s (San Jose–Oakland–Sacramento–Roseville); Washington-based corridor trains between Eugene, Oregon, and Vancouver, British Columbia (today called *Cascades*); and the ever-popular *Coast Starlight* between Los Angeles and Seattle. The Intercity unit consisted of

Mount Ascutney looms in the distance on October 21, 1997, as the southward *Vermonter* plies the Connecticut River Line at North Walpole, New Hampshire. New England Central assumed operations of the old Central Vermont in 1995. *Brian Solomon*

remaining Amtrak services, both long-distance trains and corridors.

Under the direction of Gil Mallery, Amtrak West was the most innovative unit, experimenting with a variety of new concepts and technologies. Trains such as the *Coast Starlight* were marketed as distinctive services.

Downs worked out an ambitious plan to expand Amtrak's freight services in order to reduce their federal subsidy, arranging to operate RoadRailer truck trailers on the back of its passenger trains. Although not new, RoadRailer intermodal technology had been perfected during the 1980s and obviated the need to move trailers on flatcars, allowing them to move directly on specially designed railroad

Descending from Cascade Summit through Pengra Pass on Southern Pacific's Cascade Route, Amtrak's *Coast Starlight* approaches the siding at Field, Oregon, in June 1994. Leading the train is P32BWH 513 and F40PH 251. During the mid-1990s, Amtrak's 500-series "Pepsi cans" frequently worked this train. The *Starlight* offers riders views of some of most interesting scenery in the United States, from Pacific Coast landscapes to rugged mountain vistas. *Brian Solomon*

Racing like the wind eastbound beneath the wind-ravaged volcanic slopes surrounding Avery, Washington, the short (four-car) Spokane section (Portland-Spokane) of the *Empire Builder* reflects the light of the evening sun on September 9, 2003, as it nears the former division point town of Wishram. Traveling the rails of Burlington Northern Santa Fe predecessor Spokane, Portland & Seattle, the train makes good time on this flat water-level route following the Columbia River—out of sight on the left—through the Columbia River Gorge. *Tom Kline*

wheels. This simplifies loading and unloading and reduces tare-weight, making RoadRailers preferable to traditional trailer-on-flatcars, especially when operated in conjunction with passenger equipment. Amtrak also planned to expand its fleet of express boxcars, buying both new and used cars and equipping them with high-speed trucks.

Negotiations with freight railroads did not go as smoothly as hoped, and some lines, notably Union Pacific, objected to Amtrak's freight expansion plans. However during the late 1990s, many long-distance trains began carrying increased freight traffic. For example, in November 1998, Amtrak extended its *Pennsylvanian* from a New York City–Pittsburgh run to a New York City–Chicago train, largely to carry freight and mail. This train typically resembled a freight train with rider coaches, because the freight cars greatly outnumbered the Amfleet passenger cars.

Amtrak Secures Capital Funding but Gambles Its Future

In 1997, Downs fought a two-front battle to keep Amtrak alive. He needed to secure Amtrak's reauthorization while negotiating with Amtrak's maintenance forces to circumvent a threatened strike. Furthermore in the spring of that year, Amtrak again faced a renewed cash crunch as a result of a shortfall in federal subsidy. Same story, different day. Again Amtrak looked to the states to supply additional funding to support weak-performing intercity services. The results were mixed, demonstrating the flaw in relying on states to support intercity trains that were intended as

Train No. 53, the southward *Auto Train*, marches along the old Richmond, Fredericksburg & Potomac at Ruther Glen, Virginia, on February 21, 2004. This is the heaviest and longest train on Amtrak. Behind the Superliners are the autoracks that carry passenger cars. It is routinely assigned a pair of GENESIS Series 1s (DASH 8-40BPs). *Brian Solomon*

part of a national system. As a result, Amtrak cancelled its *Desert Wind*, *Pioneer*, and, for a second time, the New Orleans–Mobile, Alabama, service, then known as the *Gulf Coast Limited*. Later in the year, following repeated threats of a total Amtrak shutdown, Congress reauthorized Amtrak's subsidy for the next five years, but with a catch: it legislated that Amtrak *must* achieve its goal of financial self-sufficiency or face liquidation proceedings. It was a politically controversial and largely impractical requirement, but one that directly shaped Amtrak's plans, operations, and outlook for the next four years.

Downs also succeeded in fending off a strike, which he believed could have destroyed Amtrak at this key juncture. In the process, he sacrificed his own job. At the end of 1997, weeks after Amtrak's appropriation was secured, Downs was effectively forced out. George Warrington, who had been CEO of the Northeast Corridor business unit, temporarily replaced him. In December 1998, Warrington was officially named Amtrak's president and CEO.

New Paradigms or New Paint?

Warrington was faced with implementing the survival strategy laid out by Downs. Amtrak finally had funding, but faced a dwindling federal subsidy as its breakeven deadline approached. Under this regime, Amtrak emphasized planned improvements in the Northeast Corridor, the introduction of new high-speed trains, further development of state-sponsored corridor services, and further growth of its mail and express business that could be used to offset passenger deficits. Shortly after becoming head of Amtrak, Warrington was quoted by Bob Johnston in *TRAINS*:

"We will not be satisfied with just reaching self-sufficiency; we can no longer exist on a survival mentality. Our absolute goal is to create a commercially based service [that's] the envy of all transportation providers."

Warrington introduced service branding and debuted new logos and a new livery for passenger equipment. The "pointless arrow" that had served since 1971 was replaced by the modern so-called "three sheets to the wind" logo. Northeast Corridor trains carried the newly devised Acela brand, a name derived from "acceleration." Ordinary NEC trains were known as *Acela Regionals*, replacing the Downs-era Northeast Direct branding. Philadelphia–New York services, traditionally known as "Clockers," were designated *Acela*

A pair of P42s leads No. 6, the *California Zephyr*, through the Truckee River Canyon near Boca Dam, California, on November 10, 2004. The F40PH was Amtrak's standard long-distance passenger locomotive for two decades before the General Electric P42 GENESIS succeeded it. A pair of P42s produce nearly as much horsepower as three F40PHs but are substantially more fuel-efficient. A P42 uses about a gallon of diesel fuel per mile when running Head End Power, roughly 30 percent less than an F40PH. *Brian Solomon*

In the 1990s, Amtrak finally extended electrification from New Haven, Connecticut, to Boston, a project that had been under discussion since before World War I. Electric services began in early 2000, and the wires are energized at the modern standard of 25 kV at 60 Hz. A number of movable bridges over waterways, such as this one at New London, Connecticut, still limit line capacity and restrict speeds on affected sections. *Brian Solomon*

Amtrak stationmaster Chuck McIntyre has been a railroader for more than two decades, and his grandfather worked in Alco's Richmond Locomotive Works. As stationmaster, he supervises ticketing, mail, express, and baggage employees, and he dispatches departing trains, such as No. 86 shown here, from Richmond, Virginia's Staples Mill Road Station. *Brian Solomon*

*Commuter*s, while the new premier high-speed service operated with specially designed high-speed trains was designated *Acela Express.* Unfortunately, this new branding confused the public, and *Acela* was often used mistakenly to identify just new high-speed trains.

Another Warrington concept was the "Satisfaction Guarantee." In the October 2000 issue of *TRAINS*, Warrington described the intent of this program: "It's not about guaranteeing an on-time train; that is not entirely in Amtrak's control. But what I can

control is an on-board experience that is positive, comforting, engaging, helpful, and feels like quality."

Wires to Boston

New Haven–Boston electrification had been

Although Amtrak no longer uses F40PHs, it still uses non-powered control units (NPCUs) rebuilt from the old diesels. A *Hiawatha* Service train approaches Sturtevant, Wisconsin, on February 8, 2002, with NPCU 90221 leading. This unit was rebuilt from F40PH 221, one of Amtrak's original 30 F40PHs built in 1976. *Hiawatha* Service trains regularly operate with push-pull equipment to simplify terminal operations. *Brian Solomon*

A passenger bids farewell before a journey on Amtrak's southward *Silver Star* boarding at Raleigh, North Carolina. The *Star* makes a late-evening stop at the North Carolina capital on its 1,431-mile journey from New York City to Miami. The trip was shorter before CSX abandoned its S Line, the old Seaboard Air Line, north of Raleigh in the late 1980s. Now, the *Star* has to make a dog leg over to the old Atlantic Coast Line route using the former Southern to Selma. As a result of this line change, Amtrak moved into the old Southern station pictured here. *Doug Koontz*

discussed for so long and so often that it seemed like a running joke in the industry. So when Amtrak finally introduced electric service to Boston in January 2000, it really was news. Initially, just a handful of daily trains ran with electric locomotives all the way to Boston. Debut of high-speed trains (HST) for *Acela Express* service was delayed because of technical problems. Limited *Acela Express* service finally began on December 10, 2000. A year later, the long-awaited *Downeaster* service—four daily roundtrips from Boston to Portland, Maine—began. It has become one of Amtrak's biggest success stories, demonstrating that corridors *do* work.

Amtrak Transcends Myth

Following four years of relative stability, Amtrak was approaching its next big financial crisis right on schedule. In the fall of 2001, Amtrak dissolved its business units on the advice of new consultants. As federal subsidy beginning to run out, it needed to trim expenses. To keep trains running, Amtrak secured a loan using New York City's Penn Station as collateral.

Amtrak's congressional mandate to reach self-sufficiency had dictated that it was not

The southward *Palmetto* sails across the massive concrete viaduct over the James River at Richmond, Virginia, on February 16, 2004. This is the former Atlantic Coast Line mainline and now CSX's primary artery for traffic moving south out of Richmond. Eight Amtrak trains use the route daily. *Brian Solomon*

Amtrak's new station at Jack London Square in Oakland, California, replaced in part the old Southern Pacific 16th Street Station that had been damaged in the 1989 Loma Prieta earthquake. Jack London Square Station and a new station at Emeryville opened in the mid-1990s. *Brian Solomon*

eligible for additional operating subsidy and that it would face liquidation if it had not attained this goal by the end of 2002. The Amtrak Reform Council, which came into being in 1997 as part of Amtrak's funding legislation, needed to make plans for Amtrak's financial failure. In early 2002, the council recommended dividing Amtrak into individual operating and infrastructure companies, a similar approach to what Britain had undertaken in the mid-1990s. (However, following a string of tragic wrecks, extreme railway congestion, the dissolution of integrated services, and increasing financial losses, observers in Britain consider the privatization of British Rail an unmitigated disaster.) By Spring 2002, Amtrak's future looked bleak and legislation was introduced in Congress to abolish the unattainable self-sufficiency requirement.

New Jersey Transit ALP46 4602 leads Amtrak Clocker train No. 627 (New York-Philadelphia) past Linden, New Jersey, on September 5, 2003. Clocker services are in transition. Traditionally, Amtrak has run these trains essentially as suburban commuter runs. As of mid-2004, NJ Transit was expected to assume full responsibility for their operation within the following few years. *Patrick Yough*

Bring in the Gunn

At this critical juncture, David Gunn, one the most experienced managers in passenger railroading, emerged from retirement to lead Amtrak. Gunn became president on May 15, 2002, and immediately began to set the railroad straight. Amtrak was perilously short of funds, and the situation was much worse than Gunn anticipated. As financial crisis loomed, he threatened to shut down the whole operation if more subsidy wasn't immediately appropriated. Five years earlier, the visions of an orderly

The great expanse of the western deserts may be best experienced by train. The *California Zephyr* works east on the old Denver & Rio Grande Western approaching the remote siding at Floy, Utah, on September 4, 1996. One of most interesting and least-explored parts of the old Rio Grande mainline is in the desert west of Grand Junction, Colorado. Although barren, the scenery is wide open and sublime in its beauty. *Brian Solomon*

dismantling of Amtrak had not taken into consideration the implications of a shutdown. As the operator of the Northeast Corridor, an Amtrak shutdown would send vital commuter-rail services into chaos, not to mention the inconvenience to the tens of thousands of

It took more than a dozen years from the time Boston-Portland, Maine, service was first seriously discussed until the first *Downeaster* trains ran on December 15, 2001. The former Boston & Maine line required substantial rehabilitation for the service, which was paid for by a mix of state and federal funding. From the start, Amtrak has operated four roundtrips daily. Rider David Clinton likes the service. "It's a regional hometown train," he says. "The crews are from Maine and they're very friendly. I like the clam chowder, too." A Boston-bound *Downeaster* crosses the Merrimack River at Haverhill, Massachusetts, on March 5, 2002. *Brian Solomon*

Amtrak's own passengers. In reality, Congress could not afford an Amtrak shutdown and found the money to keep the railroad running. Also, in the wake of events in September 2001, it was politically imprudent to deny Amtrak more subsidy: American airlines had accepted a $15 billion bailout, while Amtrak had demonstrated its value moving people during the air transport crisis. Faced with these realities, the

Bush administration softened the language calling for Amtrak's liquidation.

Gunn wasted no time in sorting out Amtrak. He reorganized management, dismissing dozens of vice presidents, while making a concerted effort to improve employee morale. Gunn rode trains systemwide and gave specific instructions for improvements based on his observations. He announced the mail and express business had been unprofitable and made plans to shut down most of these operations. He set out to clear up many of the Amtrak myths. He made it known that Amtrak's finances, long elusive, would be made public. But most importantly, he dispelled the long-held myth of Amtrak profitability. Gunn stated in a May 2003 *Railway Age* interview, "it takes enormous public investment in track, signals, equipment, and so on for a reliable system, which cannot be recovered from fares. Public dollars build airports and public dollars should build rail corridors too."

Gunn also dispelled myths that the private sector was hoping to take back Amtrak, reminding people that, "the private sector was losing millions of dollars covering passenger rail's capital and operating costs." He added that there were no quick and easy solutions to Amtrak's problems.

Through honesty about Amtrak's finances and a demonstrated willingness to meet with Amtrak's critics, Gunn improved Amtrak's credibility. He demonstrated that Amtrak was in dire need of capital investment, pointing out the poor state of infrastructure on the NEC and the desperate backlog of passenger cars awaiting repair at the Beech Grove Shops near Indianapolis.

Yet, in early 2004 as this book is being written, much of the Amtrak story remains the same: it is waiting for decisive public policy on

Above: An Amtrak F59PHI and California Cars rest between runs at Jack London Square in Oakland, California. *Fred Matthews*

Below: A pair of P42 GENESIS diesels leads No. 448, the Boston section of the *Lake Shore Limited*, east at Washington, Massachusetts, in June 2003. *Brian Solomon*

In the summer of 1989, the *Lake Shore Limited* bound for Boston passes the remnants of Boston & Albany's helper base at Chester, Massachusetts. This 1912-era coaling tower fueled steam locomotives based here to assist heavy freights over Washington Hill. Today's diesel-electric locomotives are sufficiently powerful to move trains over the B&A without help on most occasions. *Brian Solomon*

On November 2, 2003, Amtrak P32BWH 505 works a push-pull set of California Cars at Davis, California. *Brian Solomon*

its long-term role in American transport. Its ridership has reached record highs, now approaching 25 million annually, although its national market share of intercity commercial traffic has not grown significantly in years.

On the positive side, there is growing interest in the development of practical high-speed rail corridors using conventional means. Several states, such as Illinois, New York, North Carolina, and Virginia, are moving ahead with high-speed programs designed to gradually improve infrastructure to increase track speeds and lower transit times.

In spring 2004, Amtrak was still in a holding pattern. It was legislated to curtail expansion plans and focus on its existing services, but Amtrak was still waiting for sufficient funding to do its job right. In the meantime, it struggles from day to day, providing the best service it can with its meager resources.

The *Coast Starlight* poses in front of California's Mt. Shasta in 1999. *Bob Morris*

Amtrak P42 No. 1 leads the Boston section of the *Lake Shore Limited* westward through the Quaboag River Valley near West Warren, Massachusetts, in October 2000. The P42 GENESIS has become Amtrak's standard long-distance passenger locomotive. *Brian Solomon*

CHAPTER THREE

LOCOMOTIVES

Amtrak's Heritage Locomotives

In its first years Amtrak operated primarily with locomotives inherited or leased from the private railroads whose passenger service Amtrak had assumed. The diesels were largely General Motors' Electro-Motive Division (EMD) E units and F units built in the postwar period, while the electrics were primarily former Pennsylvania Railroad GG1s. By the time Amtrak began operations, most of these inherited machines were tired and nearing the end of their useful service lives. Most heritage

In its first years, Amtrak relied upon secondhand locomotives handed down from the railroads, including 198 EMD E8 and E9s, plus 13 leased from Union Pacific. On the Ides of March 1975, Amtrak 328, former Union Pacific E8A 932A, leads train No. 63, the New York City-Detroit *Empire State Express*, westward at East Rochester, New York. Many of Amtrak's E-units lasted only a few years and were bumped from service when the SDP40Fs were delivered beginning in 1973. *Doug Eisele*

locomotives were retired during Amtrak's first decade as new power was delivered, although a few E units were rebuilt to accommodate Head End Power (HEP) and survived into the mid-1980s.

EMD FL9

In 1976, Amtrak acquired 12 former New Haven Railroad FL9s as part of the complex transaction that conveyed Penn Central operations and those of other bankrupt railroads to Conrail. Of these 12 locomotives, only six were retained for service; the others were either cannibalized for parts or sold for scrap.

The model FL9 was a unique design developed by EMD to meet an unusual motive

power application. During the mid-1950s, the financially strapped New Haven Railroad desperately needed to replace its fleet of antique electric locomotives, some of which dated back to the pre–World War I period, as well as its unusual fleet of World War II–era Alco DL109 diesels. The railroad wanted to eliminate the expensive and time-consuming engine changes at New Haven and Danbury, Connecticut. The difficulty was that "off-the-shelf" diesels could not operate into New York City passenger terminals because of strict antipollution regulations in the extensive tunnels. To get around this problem, New Haven considered a proposal to remanufacture its DL109s into dual-mode units that could both draw current

in third-rail electric territory and operate under diesel-electric power. The plan was rejected in part because the modified DL109s would weigh too much for operation over the Park Avenue Viaduct approach to Grand Central Terminal.

EMD's FL9 was the solution. By lengthening a standard FP9 carbody design to 58 feet, 8 inches, EMD designed a diesel-electric/electric passenger locomotive that could either draw electric current from the 650-volt DC third rail or from its own 567 diesel engine and generator. As built, the FL9 was equipped with specialized third-rail shoes to operate on both New York Central's underrunning third rail for service to Grand Central, and on Pennsylvania Railroad's overrunning third rail in Penn Station. To accommodate light axle loads on the Park Avenue Viaduct, EMD used an A1A Flexicoil truck to support the rear of the locomotive.

In the New Haven–era, FL9s were largely assigned to Boston–New York and Springfield–New York long-distance trains. Following changes that resulted from the transition to Penn Central and then Amtrak, the FL9 fleet was assigned new duties. Amtrak preferred a Penn Station routing for Boston –New York trains. The operation of through Boston–Washington, D.C., services effectively eliminated the need to assign FL9s to Boston trains. During Penn Central, most FL9s had been reassigned to Grand Central suburban runs on former New York Central Hudson and Harlem lines, as well as on former New Haven Railroad lines. In the mid-1970s, Amtrak assigned its FL9 fleet to Empire Corridor trains to simplify operations into Grand Central by eliminating the need for an engine change at Croton-Harmon (at the end of third-rail territory).

According to the August 1989 issue of *Passenger Train Journal,* in 1979 and 1980 Amtrak sent six FL9s to Boise, Idaho, for re-building by Morrison-Knudsen. In their book *Diesels to Park Avenue,* authors Joe Snopek

Amtrak FL9 488 leads an Albany-bound train at Breakneck Ridge, near Cold Spring, New York, on November 20, 1992. Amtrak's fleet of former New Haven FL9s primarily worked Empire Corridor trains between New York City and Albany–Rensselaer. Between 1990 and 1993, Amtrak overhauled its FL9 fleet at Beech Grove, Indiana. Among the changes was the replacement of 16-567 diesel engines with more modern 16-645E engines. *Brian Solomon*

and Robert A. La May list more than 20 alterations made to Amtrak's FL9s. Among the more significant was their adaptation to supply Head End Power, which was required

to operate with Amfleet and other modern Amtrak passenger equipment. These locomotives were numbered 485 through 489 and 491 (this unit was later renumbered 484).

Between 1990 and 1993, Amtrak overhauled its FL9 fleet at Beech Grove, Indiana. According to Snopek and La May, among the changes made during this overhaul was the replacement of model 567 diesel engines with more-modern 645E engines.

In later years Amtrak's six FL9s were the last traditional EMD passenger cabs on the railroad. They worked in regular service on New York–Albany Empire Corridor trains until the mid-1990s. (Occasionally, an FL9 would stray toward Buffalo.) In 1991, Amtrak ended regular operations to Grand Central Terminal in favor of a new routing via Manhattan's West Side Line to Penn Station. Amtrak replaced the FL9s with new 700-series, General Electric (GE) P32AC-DM dual-mode GENESIS units. The first 700-series GENESIS arrived in Albany–Rensselaer in September 1995 and gradually displaced the FL9s from revenue service.

During 1973 and 1974, EMD built 150 SDP40Fs for Amtrak at total cost of $65 million. They were numbered from 500 to 649 and were delivered as part of two orders. Nos. 558 and 569 lead train No. 13, the Seattle-bound *Coast Starlight*, on the Southern Pacific at Santa Susana Pass in Chatsworth, California, on February 18, 1977. Note the flat nose section on 558, which identifies the locomotive as part of the second order. The first 40 had slightly pointed noses. *Brian Jennison*

On April 19, 1980, three SDP40Fs work eastward on the Santa Fe at Streator, Illinois, with train No. 4, the *Southwest Limited*. This photo was made toward the end of the Amtrak's steam-heat era. Within two years, F40PHs and Superliners were the standard consist on most western long-distance trains. SDP40F 500 pictured here was the first in the series and was traded back to EMD in the early 1980s as credit on F40PHRs. *Steve Smedley*

Amtrak ordered 25 P30CHs from General Electric in June 1974. These were Amtrak's first diesels equipped with HEP and were designed to operate with Amfleet, purchased concurrently. In their early years, the P30CH fleet (700 through 724) was based at Woodcrest, Illinois, and Ivy City, Washington, D.C., for maintenance. On St. Patrick's Day 1977, 715 leads train No. 33, the westward *Shenandoah*, across the Potomac River at Harpers Ferry, West Virginia, on the Baltimore & Ohio. *George Kowanski*

New Amtrak Locomotives

As the primary provider of long-distance passenger service, Amtrak is in an unusual position when it comes to locomotive acquisition. Unlike the freight railroads, which can place large orders of off-the-shelf models, Amtrak requires smaller numbers of specially designed machines. The result is that Amtrak must pay a higher cost for each new locomotive. Amtrak has used two strategies: buying freight locomotives adapted by the manufacturer for passenger service, or paying for the design of specialized locomotives. Initially, Amtrak chose the former option with mixed results. Its early locomotive purchases are not generally well regarded. As a result, in recent times Amtrak has tended toward specialized designs. Although Amtrak is not the only market for passenger locomotives (commuter agencies and the Canadian passenger operator VIA Rail also buy new power), it has tended to set trends in North American passenger locomotive development. One aspect of Amtrak's modern locomotive purchases has been the introduc-

Amtrak SDP40F 576 leads train No. 10, the eastward *North Coast Hiawatha*, across the Mississippi River at Minneapolis on March 1, 1975. The *North Coast Hiawatha* was a tri-weekly Chicago-Seattle train that operated from June 1971 until October 1979. Its name reflected its historic route. Between Chicago and Minneapolis, it used the Milwaukee Road mainline, once the route of the *Hiawatha*; west of Minneapolis it largely followed the old Northern Pacific line, once the route of NP's *North Coast Limited*. The old Great Northern Stone Arch Bridge pictured here was built in 1883 and was removed from service in 1981. *John Gruber*

tion of European technology. Where North American locomotive builders GE and EMD are world leaders in freight diesel designs, the relatively low demand for American and Canadian passenger locomotives has resulted in European manufacturers leading the way in this area. In Europe, the demand for passenger power greatly outweighs the need for freight diesels.

Passenger locomotives need to accelerate faster and operate at higher top speeds than freight locomotives. At the same time, they are not required to haul as much tonnage. Adjusting the top speed of a locomotive is accomplished by changing the gear ratio

In 1978, F40PHs 224 and 223 are bound for San Diego on the Santa Fe with *San Diegan* service No. 776 at Del Mar, California. EMD F40PHs, the first 30 of which were delivered in 1976, were Amtrak's workhorses for two decades. These 3,000-horsepower, four-axle locomotives had 40-inch wheels and could deliver a continuous 38,240-pound tractive effort at 16 miles per hour. Most were geared for 103-miles-per-hour maximum speed. *Fred Matthews*

between the traction motors and the axles. Higher operating speeds may also require the use of specialized trucks to maintain adequate wheel–rail contact and to prevent derailments. Passenger locomotives also need to provide heating and lighting to passenger cars. Traditionally heating was provided with a steam generator and electricity generated on the passenger cars, but since the mid-1970s, Amtrak has invested in locomotives and cars that use electrically powered heating and lighting drawing current supplied by the locomotive. This system is known as Head End Power (HEP); the power is either generated by the locomotive's prime mover (onboard diesel engine used primarily for traction) or by an auxiliary diesel. As a result, passenger loco-

motives require more equipment than freight locomotives and have more elaborate electrical systems that require additional engineering. A drawback to HEP systems is that when complexity is added to a locomotive design there are more opportunities for problems to develop.

Another difference with passenger locomotives is aesthetics. Since the 1950s, freight locomotives have been largely utilitarian designs. Passenger locomotives, on the other hand, need to look good and the public has come to expect a more streamlined appearance. As a result, aesthetics is taken into greater consideration in passenger locomotive design. Whether the public agrees with the tastes of the designer or not is a separate issue. Amtrak has dictated aesthetic concerns to the manufacturers of several of its recent locomotive designs—the GENESIS and *Acela Express* high-speed trains (HSTs) were designed to please Amtrak in both performance and appearance.

Complicating the ordering process is

The first order of F40PHs were built in 1976 and numbered in the 200 series to commemorate the American bicentennial. The class leader leads train 448, the *Lake Shore Limited*, down Washington Hill through the Twin Ledges near Middlefield, Massachusetts. *Brian Solomon*

In March 1986, the Sunday-scheduled *Charter Oak* (Boston-Washington, D.C., via Springfield, Massachusetts) races west through West Brookfield, Massachusetts. West Brookfield has some of America's oldest remaining railroad structures. The Western Railroad freight house (right) dates from the 1840s, while the "old" passenger station (not pictured) dates from the late 1830s. The "new" passenger station (left of the train) was built in the 1890s. Today, it serves as a senior center. *Brian Solomon*

Amtrak's inherently political nature. Amtrak's creation was political, its route structure is dictated in part by political considerations, its ongoing funding has political implications, and consequentially locomotive (and other equipment) acquisitions may be influenced by political agendas. As a result, the most effective equipment from a technical standpoint is not always the simplest solution for Amtrak.

Electro-Motive SDP40F

Amtrak's first new diesel locomotives were an order of 40 SDP40Fs from Electro-Motive delivered in June 1973. Amtrak's SDP40Fs were six-axle/six-motor locomotives powered by EMD's proven 16-cylinder 645E3 diesel engine rated at 3,000 horsepower. The SDP40F was essentially an adaptation of EMD's very successful SD40-2 freight locomotive, which used a covered cowl design. (EMD's first

application of the cowl was in 1968 on nine FP45s built for Santa Fe—locomotives that were very similar to the SDP40F. The FP45 was rated at 3,600 horsepower and used a 20-cylinder 645 engine.)

The SDP40F was 3 feet, 6 inches longer than the standard SD40-2, measuring 72 feet 4 inches. At 396,000 pounds, they were significantly heavier, as well. The model was geared for a top speed of 103 miles per hour and designed for long-distance service. At the time the locomotives were ordered, Amtrak's intercity passenger car fleet was still entirely equipped for steam heat (a carryover from the steam era), and as a result the SDP40Fs were fitted with a pair of Vapor OK-4625 steam generators. Water was stored both in below-frame tanks divided to accommodate diesel fuel and water (2,850 and 2,150 gallons, respectively) and in round 1,350-gallon tanks

located forward of the steam generators inside the engine compartment. It was anticipated that SDP40Fs would be eventually converted to HEP, and at least some of the locomotives had provision for HEP, although none were ever so-equipped on Amtrak.

Amtrak's SDP40Fs were initially assigned to the *Super Chief*, where they followed on the heels of Santa Fe's FP45s, bought for essentially the same service. (After Amtrak took over Santa Fe's passenger services, Santa Fe reassigned its FP45s to freight.)

Four months after the first order, Amtrak ordered another 110 SDP40Fs. The total cost of 150 locomotives was $65 million and they were numbered from 500 to 649. The two orders were very similar, except for minor differences such as the nose profile. The earlier locomotives featured a slightly pointed nose, like the FP45s, while the later locomotives

had a flat front. Some units in the earlier order were also slightly taller, which resulted in some operating restrictions.

Early on, locomotive engineers noted that SDP40s exhibited excessive lateral swaying, which seemed most pronounced on poorer track. Within a few years of their delivery the SDP40Fs were involved in a number of derailments. According to the March 1977 *Railway Gazette International*, a December 16, 1976, derailment of the *San Francisco Zephyr* on Burlington Northern (BN) trackage led that railroad to impose a 40-mile-per-hour speed restriction on SDP40Fs traversing sharp curves. BN believed the cause of derailments was a result of SDP40Fs spreading the track gauge. A month later, SDP40s were involved in another serious derailment on Louisville & Nashville trackage that resulted in the National Transportation Safety Board

The *Pioneer* ran from Seattle to Chicago via Denver. In eastern Oregon it crossed a succession of three serious grades on the Union Pacific: Kamela Summit, Telocassett Hill, and Encina Hill. Amtrak No. 26, the eastward *Pioneer*, descends Encina Hill at Pleasant Valley, Oregon, in July 1991, behind F40PH 410. Budget cuts killed this service in May 1997. *Brian Solomon*

In the early 1990s, a pair of Amtrak F40PHs leads the *Reno Fun Train* westward through the Truckee River Canyon at Floriston, California, on the eastern slope of Southern Pacific's famous crossing of Donner Pass. This train comprised former Santa Fe Bi-level passenger cars built for service on its *El Capitan.* Parallel to the railroad is Interstate 80, which runs from the George Washington Bridge to the San Francisco Bay Bridge. *Brian Solomon*

recommending that SDP40Fs (and GE P30CHs) operate at restricted speeds through curves. These restrictions caused numerous delays because trains assigned SDP40Fs could not maintain schedules.

As a result of 17 suspect SDP40F derailments, Amtrak, the American Association of Railroads, various freight railroads, and EMD participated in extensive testing to determine the cause of the derailments. These tests were inconclusive, but a variety of theories emerged. The lateral swaying may have been caused by a combination of the high water tanks (and water sloshing inside them) and the use of hollow-bolster HT-C six-motor trucks at higher speeds. A related problem may have been the condition of the tracks, as derailments did not occur on lines with excellent track standards.

The SDP40F's problems emerged at an especially inopportune time for Amtrak, politically. By early 1977, Congress' impatience with Amtrak's growing costs was leading to talks of restructuring the railroad. Regardless of the cause, the SDP40Fs were tainted by the derailments and gave Amtrak a bad reputation with freight railroads, the public, and politicians. A quick fix was needed.

Amtrak had already ordered its first four-motor F40PHs from EMD for service with the new HEP Amfleet. Like the SDP40Fs,

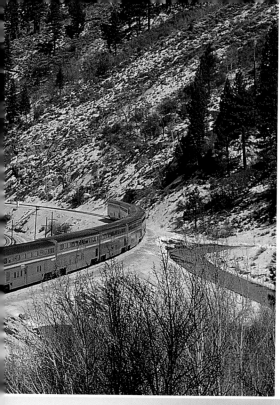

these were adapted from a freight locomotive design, but used a variation of the proven four-axle Blomberg truck design, were not equipped with steam boilers, and, most significantly, had not experienced derailments. By mid-1977, Amtrak basically gave up on the SDP40F, eventually trading most of them back to EMD for F40PHs. The decision was also influenced by the success of HEP, which performed much better than steam heat

At sunset on December 16, 1988, the eastward *Maple Leaf* from Toronto to New York, train No. 64, approaches DeWitt, New York, on Conrail's former New York Central Water Level Route. The F40PHs with Amfleet were standard equipment on this run until 2002. At Albany–Rensselaer, F40PHs were exchanged for FL9s (and later dual-mode GENESIS) for the run down the Hudson Line to New York City. *Brian Solomon*

Amtrak F40PH 287 leads the *Vermonter* across the Quaboag at Three Rivers, Massachusetts. In its first few years the *Vermonter* carried a distinctively painted baggage car that was removed from the train in 2002. *Michael L. Gardner*

during the tough winter of 1976 and 1977. (The preference for F40PHs accelerated Amtrak's switch to HEP. Not only was it used on all subsequent passenger car orders, but it resulted in the conversion of older heritage cars, as well.) The SDP40Fs survived on some long-distance trains until 1981. By this time, most had been exchanged for new F40PHs and the steam-heat era had nearly come to a close. In 1984, Amtrak traded its 18 remaining SDP40Fs to Santa Fe for a fleet of 25 CF7

The northward *Vermonter* rumbles across the Millers Falls High Bridge, in Millers Falls, Massachusetts, in June 2003. This train was one of the last that Amtrak regularly assigned F40PHs. Now, as pictured here, it runs with GENESIS diesels. *Brian Solomon*

road switchers (rebuilt by the railroad from EMD F7s) and SSB1200 switchers (rebuilt from SW1200s). These SDP40Fs were modified by Santa Fe and worked road freights through the 1990s.

P30CH

In 1974, Amtrak ordered 25, 3,000-horsepower cowl locomotives from GE, designated P30CH, at a cost of $480,000 each. These boxy-looking machines, nicknamed "Pooches" by crews and fans alike, measured 72 feet, 4 inches long; 10 feet, 8.8 inches wide; and 15 feet, 4.5 inches tall; and weighed 386,000 pounds. They were derived from GE's U30C freight locomotive and used GE's standard 16-cylinder 7FDL engine to supply power for traction motors. The P30CHs were Amtrak's first diesels with HEP, which was generated by twin auxiliary diesel engine generator sets. The P30CHs were orphans on Amtrak and for many years the only GE diesels in regular revenue passenger service. In later years some were assigned to Lorton, Virginia–Sanford, Florida, *Auto Train* service and to the *Sunset*, Amtrak's tri-weekly run over Southern Pacific's Sunset Route between New Orleans and Los Angeles.

EMD F40PH

The powerful F40PH diesel-electric is often called "the diesel that saved Amtrak." This 3,000-horsepower four-axle, four-motor loco-motive was originally ordered in early 1976 for short-haul operations. When Amtrak abandoned the SDP40F, the F40PH became Amtrak's workhorse diesel and was assigned to all types of passenger services (outside exclu-sively electrified zones in the Northeast). Between 1976 and 1987, Amtrak ordered a total of 210 F40PHs from EMD. The initial batch was numbered 200 to 229 to honor the American bicentennial and were painted with red, white, and blue stripes. Later locomotives, many of which were built as trades from the SDP40Fs, were designated F40PHRs. Amtrak's fleet was numbered sequentially from 200 to 409. An additional group of six F40PHs was acquired secondhand from Ontario's GO Transit commuter agency and carried Amtrak numbers 410 to 415.

EMD adapted the F40PH model from its successful GP40-2 freight locomotive and incorporated the cowl covering. Other differ-ences were the HEP generator and related electrical alterations. Amtrak's F40PHs were powered by variations of the 16-cylinder 645E3

The Boston–Portland, Maine, *Downeaster* trains are operated with push-pull equipment. On the Portland end, an 800-series GENESIS provides power, and on the Boston end is a non-powered control units (NPCU) "Cabbage" specially painted for the service. In the mid-1990s, Amtrak converted 21 of its old F40PHs into unpowered cab-control cars. No. 90214, seen here on March 5, 2002, at Rockingham Junction, New Hampshire, was originally F40PH 214. *Brian Solomon*

Against the backdrop of the Chicago skyline, train No. 347, the *Illinois Zephyr*, approaches Roosevelt Road shortly after its departure from Union Station. Leading the train is locomotive 192, a former GO Transit GP40TC. Amtrak acquired eight of these locomotives (192 through 199) from the Canadian commuter agency in 1988. They were built in London, Ontario, in 1966 by General Motors Diesel Ltd., EMD's Canadian subsidiary. A longer frame was needed to accommodate an auxiliary diesel and alternator to supply HEP. *Brian Solomon*

engine (also used in the SDP40F). Most used a 57:20 gear ratio for a top speed of 103 miles per hour, while Nos. 329 to 360 were built with a 56:21 gear ratio for a 110-mile-per-hour top speed. An auxiliary generator powered by the 645 diesel engine produced HEP. According to Amtrak's F40PH/P30CH operating manual of 1983, the F40PH's HEP generator was controlled by the engineer and had three positions: normal, standby, and isolate(d). In the normal position, the 645 engine operated at a maximum speed (893 rpm), even when the locomotive was stationary. For this reason,

the F40PHs were extremely noisy when standing at stations. In the standby position, engine speed was 720 rpm, much faster than the ordinary idle speed. Since engine speed is governed to generate HEP, when in normal HEP mode, the throttle was used only to excite the main generator to control electrical supply to traction motors, rather than the typical diesel-electric control arrangement that matched engine speed to generator output.

Despite the HEP system, F40PHs were relatively simple locomotives. They proved to be powerful and reliable performers that served Amtrak for the better part of two decades. Had it not been for their reliability, Amtrak may have had a far more difficult time justifying its continued existence during times of federal budget cuts. The locomotives were popular with

locomotive engineers, too, because of their rapid throttle response and acceleration.

Amtrak's F40PHs were gradually phased out with the purchase of GENESIS and F59PHI locomotives and the extension of Northeast Corridor electrification to Boston. Among the final regular assignments for F40PHs were on Springfield–Hartford–New Haven shuttles, and on the *Maple Leaf*, which for part of its journey was run with Canadian crews who, until delivery of VIA Rail's GENESIS units in 2002, were unfamiliar with the operation of these newer units.

In the mid-1990s, Amtrak rebuilt 21 of its F40PHs into cab-control and cab/baggage cars. (Designated by Amtrak as non-powered control units [NPCU], the latter are known colloquially as "Cabbages.") NPCUs have been

General Electric built 20 DASH 8-32BWHs for Amtrak in 1991. On the evening of January 17, 1993, No. 519, the highest in the series, pauses with Amtrak train No. 5 at Southern Pacific's Sparks, Nevada, yard for a station stop and a crew change. Brutal winter conditions on Donner Pass delayed arrival of the train. Today, Amtrak largely uses these GEs for secondary service and as switchers. *Brian Solomon*

The *Downeaster* crosses the Salmon Falls Bridge north of Dover, New Hampshire, in March 2002. Leading is GENESIS Series 1 DASH 8-40BP No. 809, wearing the Northeast Direct paint livery. This has been a regular assignment for the older GENESIS diesels. *Brian Solomon*

regularly assigned to push-pull train-sets used on the *Downeaster*, *Hiawatha*, Chicago–Detroit Corridor, and *Cascades* services. By the end of 2003, Amtrak had sold, converted, or retired virtually all of its F40PHs.

In the late 1980s Amtrak tested some pioneer three-phase, AC-traction diesel-electrics. In 1987, F40PH No. 202 was rebuilt by Brown-Boveri. Later, Amtrak tested a pair of experimental EMD F69PH-ACs built lin 1988. Today, most Amtrak diesels still use traditional DC-traction motors, although all of its new electrics use three-phase AC traction, as do GE's dual-mode GENESIS locomotives discussed later in this chapter.

General Electric DASH 8-32BWH

In 1991, Amtrak acquired 20 DASH 8-32BWH (Amtrak designated them P32BH) locomotives from GE, based on Santa Fe's 500 series that GE built in 1990. Amtrak's locomotives share most external dimensions with Santa Fe's 500s, but feature several significant internal differences, namely GE's 12-cylinder FDL engine instead of the 16-cylinder used on the Santa Fe. The 12-cylinder FDL is used to produce 3,200 horsepower for traction, and it drives an auxiliary alternator for HEP (represented by "H" in the designation). Amtrak numbered its DASH 8-32BWHs in the 500 series, the block of numbers previously occupied by the SDP40Fs. Also with the DASH 8-32BWH, Amtrak introduced an entirely new paint scheme that observers compared to that used by Pepsi on its 12-ounce aluminum cola cans, leading to the unofficial moniker "Pepsi Cans." These locomotives were often assigned to Amtrak's West Coast services (two were financed by Caltrans and carried state markings) and were commonly used on California's *San Joaquins*

and *Capitols*, as well as on the *Coast Starlight*, *California Zephyr*, and *Southwest Chief*. In modern times they are assigned standby service, switcher duties, and work as seasonal trains like the ever-popular "Reno Fun Train."

General Electric GENESIS

By the early 1990s, Amtrak's fleet of EMD F40PHs was approaching retirement age and the railroad sought to replace them with a new design. Amtrak wanted a modern, lightweight state-of-the-art passenger locomotive that was more than a mere adaptation of freight designs. Both GE and EMD placed bids for

the new type. Amtrak's specification for the new machine was AMD-103, which indicated *Am*trak *Di*esel and a 103-mile-per-hour maximum speed. Ultimately, GE won the contract and worked with Amtrak to develop a completely new design that incorporated several European concepts. To provide a suitable name for new the machine, GE held an employee contest that produced the GENESIS brand name. So far, Amtrak has ordered three different GENESIS models.

GENESIS is unique in the annals of modern American locomotives. Unlike other modern diesels, GENESIS is specifically designed for North American passenger services and is fundamentally different from modern freight locomotives. Instead of a bottom-supporting locomotive platform and cast trucks, GENESIS uses an integral monocoque body shell and fabricated trucks, both designs that incorporate technology derived from modern European practice rather than traditional North American practice. The fabricated trucks use a high-tractive-effort, lightweight, bolsterless design that appears significantly different than contemporary locomotive trucks.

Amtrak specified a powerful and fuel-efficient locomotive that was significantly lighter and more compact than available models. GE worked with Krupp—the German firm responsible for DB AG's (German State Railway) high-speed ICE-1 body design—in the construction of the monocoque body shell that is integral to the locomotive structure. In this respect, GENESIS is like the full carbody locomotives built in the 1930s, 1940s, and 1950s.

Also, because Amtrak wanted a locomotive that complied with the most restrictive mainline clearances, GENESIS is lower and narrower than typical North American road locomotives: GENESIS Series 1 measures 14 feet, 6 inches tall and 10 feet wide.

Amtrak No. 88 crosses the Rapidan River at Fredericksburg, Virginia, at 9:41 a.m. on February 22, 2004. Externally, Amtrak's P42s are very similar to the other GENESIS models. Most primary components are the ame as in the earlier DASH 8-40BP, but the P42DC uses GE's more advanced DASH 9 technology with features such as electronic fuel injection for improved performance. The P42DC is capable of 110 miles per hour. *Brian Solomon*

Perhaps the most striking quality of GE's GENESIS line, however, is its unorthodox appearance. Amtrak designer Cesar Vergara avoided complex curves and instead used angular construction with flat surfaces. Vergara, who has enjoyed a prolific career in railroad industrial design, also developed the original GENESIS paint livery. GENESIS has won awards for industrial design, and today

Continued on page 114

Passengers aboard train No. 8, the *Empire Builder*, enjoy views of a winter wonderland east of Montana's Glacier National Park on February 16, 2000. Leading the train is a pair of GENESIS Series 1 DASH 8-40BPs in the Northeast Direct paint livery. These locomotives numbered in the 800 series were the first of three GENESIS models bought by Amtrak. They use GE's DASH 8 technology, including the 7FDL-16 prime mover rated at 4,000 horsepower, the GMG 195A1 alternator, and four GE752AH8 traction motors. *Don Marson*

Amtrak P32AC-DM No. 704 leads a westbound Empire Corridor train at Guy Park, west of Amsterdam, New York. The dual-mode GENESIS use a three-phase AC traction system instead of the more conventional DC traction used by most Amtrak diesel-electrics. A single GMG 199 alternator supplies power for both traction and HEP. Four inverters supply three-phase that powers four GEB15 AC-traction motors for propulsion. *Brian Solomon*

North Carolina DOT bought a pair of F59PHIs in 1998 for use on the state-sponsored *Piedmont* (Raleigh-Charlotte). Named *City of Salisbury* and *City of Asheville*, these F59PHIs carry road numbers that represent the founding dates of those cities. On February 19, 2004, 1755 *City of Salisbury* leads Amtrak's *Piedmont* at Spencer. The locomotive's paint scheme incorporates the colors and design of the state flag. *Brian Solomon*

This view (right) depicts the cab interior of North Carolina DOT F59PHI 1797 *City of Asheville*, a locomotive that features EMD's Isolated Cab in which noise levels are limited to 66 decibels when idling and 86 decibels at maximum throttle (known as "Run-8," the highest of eight throttle positions), compared to 100 decibels in locomotives with traditional cab designs. The F59PHI is equipped with modern desktop controls that allow the engineer to face forward. *Brian Solomon*

Vergara is one of the most respected names in the industry.

All three variations of GENESIS diesels use the same basic monocoque shell. However, while they appear nearly identical externally, they feature significant internal differences. The first type were the GENESIS Series 1, rated at 4,000 horsepower and designated as DASH 8-40BP by GE and as P40 by Amtrak. Forty-four were built at GE's Erie, Pennsylvania, shops between 1993 and 1994, and they are numbered in the 800 series. The type debuted in Amtrak service in June 1993, with Nos. 802 and 804 used on the Virginia-Florida *Autotrain*.

GENESIS Series 1 locomotives use GE's DASH 8-era technology. With a 74:29 gear ratio, they are geared for 103 miles per hour maximum speed, but in actual service are rarely required to run faster than 90 miles per hour. (A 79-mile-per-hour maximum speed is typical for passenger trains on most American mainlines, unless equipped with advanced signaling systems.)

GE adopted Amtrak's designation scheme for later GENESIS types. Today, the more common GENESIS is the 4,200-horsepower model P42DC. Amtrak's fleet began production in 1996 and is numbered 1 to 207.

Amtrak's third GENESIS variation is the 700 series P32AC-DMs. These specialized machines are designed for service on third-rail electrified lines in New York City. Known as "dual-mode" locomotives (accounting for the "DM" in the designation), they are the modern-day successor to EMD's FL9. The P32AC-DM is powered by GE's 12-cylinder 7FDL diesel engine, but using retractable third-rail shoes, the units can draw direct current from trackside third rail. Because the P32AC-DMs are specialized locomotives, they are exclusively used in Empire Corridor services to New York's Penn Station, although they have made occasional trips to Grand Central Terminal as the result of detours.

Electro-Motive F59PHI

California's commitment to funding statewide

passenger services led it to order a distinctive fleet of locomotives to haul its Amtrak-run trains. At a time when Amtrak was looking to GE to supply a new fleet of long-distance passenger power, California worked with General Motors' Electro-Motive Division to develop a contemporary equivalent to the successful F40PH locomotive. To meet California's requirements, EMD adapted its F59PH, which had been developed for suburban rail service. The result was a powerful, modern-looking streamlined diesel-electric that complied with strict California emission requirements. Designated F59PHI, it was EMD's first streamlined diesel built for the American market in a generation. Its appearance was a strong contrast to the utilitarian designs that had prevailed on American railroads since the late 1950s and very different from GE's recently debuted GENESIS line.

Passenger Train Journal reported that Caltrans ordered the first nine F59PHI's in January 1993 at a cost of $20.8 million.

Numbered 2001 to 2009, they were delivered in 1994. Primary components were constructed at EMD's La Grange, Illinois, plant, where most of its traditional locomotives for the U.S. market had been made, but final assembly was done at its London, Ontario, plant.

The F59PHI designation indicates the locomotives are designed for passenger service with HEP and that they have EMD's Isolated Cab design intended to reduce cab noise and vibrations. Primary components of the "59" series include a 12-cylinder 710G3 diesel engine (EMD's latest design at that time), an AR15 alternator, and D87B series traction motors. The F59PHI engine uses electronic fuel injection, and the locomotive is rated at 3,200 horsepower. Like GE's 1970s-era P30CH, the F59PHI uses an auxiliary engine and alternator for HEP, which offers several advantages over drawing HEP from the prime mover, as in the F40PHs. The auxiliary HEP diesel allows the main engine to idle at a lower throttle notch, thus saving fuel and reducing wear and tear on the main engine,

In December 1998, F59PHI No. 460 waits in the morning gloom at Seattle with the *Leavenworth Snow Train*, an excursion that will ascend Burlington Northern Santa Fe's Stevens Pass. This train comprised 14 cars, mostly Amfleet I, and F59PHIs at both ends to simplify reversing the train at Wenatchee, Washington. *Brian Solomon*

The General Electric E60CHs were primarily used in later years for hauling long-distance services on the Northeast Corridor. Long-distance trains, such as No. 19, the *Crescent*, seen here at Elizabeth, New Jersey, on February 9, 2002, operate on slower schedules between New York and Washington, D.C., than services designed to cater to the Northeast market. Also, a single E60CH had the ability to provide head-end power to a long consist more reliably than a single AEM-7. *Patrick Yough*

while producing less noise. When the train is moving, the HEP does not draw power from the main engine, thus allowing more power for propulsion.

The F59PHI measures 58 feet, 2 inches long; 15 feet, 11.5 inches tall; and 10 feet, 6 inches wide; and weighs 270,000 pounds. The California locomotives were designed with a 56:21 gear ratio, which would allow them to operate at a top speed of 110 miles per hour. However, most of the lines on which they are routinely run are equipped with signaling systems that allow for a maximum speed of only 79 miles per hour.

The locomotive is shrouded in a cowl, which primarily serves an aesthetic function, although the F59PHI's aerodynamic design also reduces wind resistance. The bulbous nose is constructed from fiberglass composite, and below it are thick steel plates to protect the crew. Together, the nose and plates offer greater strength than the traditional stream-lined "bulldog" nose used on EMD's famous E- and F-units.

EMD's Isolated Cab was first used on its heavy-haul freight locomotives and was offered as an option through the 1990s. Unlike traditional designs, with the cab built as part of the rest of the locomotive, the Isolated Cab has a separate structure and is connected to the locomotive using rubber pads designed to retard noise and vibration, thus providing a more pleasant working environment for the crews. The first nine F59PHIs were painted in the Amtrak California livery featuring dark blue, gold, and metallic silver. Amtrak received an additional 20 locomotives in 1997, which carry different liveries, including the cream, forest green, and a shade of brown

The AEM-7 has been the Northeast Corridor (NEC) workhorse since the early 1980s, effectively assuming the duties long held by the Pennsylvania Railroad's famous GG1. On February 3, 1996, AEM-7 940 races along the NEC at Prospect Park, Pennsylvania, with train No. 95. The AEM-7 was derived from Sweden's Rc4, a type designed for freight and passenger service. Many Rc models remain in service in Sweden, and related types are used in many other countries. *David Palmer*

Amtrak AEM-7 AC 923 leads a westward *Acela Regional* service at New London, Connecticut, in October 2002. The New Haven-Boston electrification was completed in 2000 and uses 25 kV at 60 Hz. Don't let the AEM-7's small size deceive you: this is an extremely powerful machine, capable of maintaining 125 miles per hour with an eight-car train. *Brian Solomon*

known as "cappuccino" used on Washington's and Oregon's *Cascades*.

The North Carolina Department of Transportation (NCDOT) piggybacked an order for two F59PHIs on a larger Amtrak order. Built in February 1998, these two units are used on the intrastate *Piedmont*, operated by Amtrak but funded by NCDOT. These are the only F59PHIs operating on Amtrak trains in the eastern United States. In addition to the locomotives for Amtrak services, several North American commuter agencies have also ordered the F59PHI.

Although the F59PHI is a relatively unusual type in the United States, similar locomotives have been built for operations overseas. Much of the same equipment used in the F59PHI was adapted for Irish Rail's Class 201 (EMD Model JT42HCW), a dual-service,

six-motor, double-cab diesel built for 5-foot, 3-inch-gauge tracks.

Amtrak Electrics

Amtrak has operated on overhead electrified lines of the former New Haven and Pennsylvania railroads since it began operations in 1971. This is the Northeast Corridor and Amtrak's busiest and most heavily traveled route. In addition to the New Haven-New York City-Washington, D.C., trunk, Amtrak has also operated electrically powered services on the Philadelphia-Harrisburg line and briefly on the Port Road along the Susquehanna River. Today, electric services operate all the way to Boston, while most Harrisburg services are diesel-hauled. Although the Boston-Washington, D.C., route uses high-voltage, single-phase AC overhead electrification, the voltage and frequency parameters vary as a result of the Northeast Corridor's complex history (i.e., when various segments were electrified and by whom).

General Electric E60C

In 1973, Amtrak ordered new, six-axle, six-motor electrics from GE to replace the aging GG1 fleet. To suit Amtrak's needs, without having to design an entirely new machine, GE adapted a single-ended freight electric type designated E60C that had been built for Arizona's Black Mesa & Lake Powell a few years earlier. Like the SDP40F, F40PH, and GE's P30CH diesels, the E60Cs used a cowl covering. Ultimately, GE built a fleet of 26 double-ended, high-horsepower electrics designated E60CP and E60CH. These un-adorned, flat-fronted machines were dressed in Amtrak's red, blue, and silver ("platinum mist") scheme.

According to *The Contemporary Diesel Spotter's Guide* by Louis Marre and Jerry Pinkepank, the E60CP used a steam generator for traditional steam-heated passenger equipment, while the E60CHs were equipped with HEP for use with the new Amfleet cars. Frank Wilner notes in *The Amtrak Story* that each locomotive cost $692,000. They were built for 120-mile-per-hour service and produced 6,000 horsepower. However a high-speed derailment that occurred in the final days of testing revealed that the E60CP and E60CH used a truck design potentially inadequate for high-speed operation—when running at high speeds the trucks placed excessive lateral forces on rails. This problem delayed delivery of the locomotives and when they finally did arrive, instead of the intended 120 miles per hour, a speed limit of just 85 miles per hour was imposed to avoid derailments. Unsatisfied with the E60C's lower speed, Amtrak looked overseas for a more effective high-speed electric. In the early 1980s Amtrak sold off surplus E60s to suburban passenger operator NJ Transit and the Navajo Mine, a mining railway in New Mexico. Amtrak retained some E60Cs, which were renumbered in the 600 series and remained in regular service on heavy long-distance trains (using the Northeast Corridor) between New York and Washington, D.C.

Amtrak HHP8 (sometimes designated HHL) No. 660 leads an *Acela Regional* train at North Rahway, New Jersey, on June 8, 2001. *Patrick Yough*

The last of the type were finally retired at the end of 2003.

AEM-7

The unsuccessful experiences with E60Cs in high-speed service led Amtrak to look to Europe for a more effective design. The company imported both a French six-motor electric and a Swedish Rc4 electric for Northeast Corridor testing. The latter proved the preferred machine.

The Rc type was developed in the 1960s and was the first commercial locomotive to employ thyristor (semiconductor) motor control. The development of thyristor motor control represented an electronic advancement over traditional electromechanical or pneumatic motor control by providing stepless traction motor regulation, allowing for maximum motor output without wheel slip.

The result is greater tractive effort and improved efficiency.

Amtrak was pleased with the Rc and ordered a derivative locomotive designated AEM-7 that was assembled by EMD at La Grange, Illinois, under license. Although the AEM-7 resembles its Swedish prototypes, it has a tougher body shell in order to comply with American safety requirements and is significantly more powerful in order to reach higher speeds. The AEM-7 delivers 53,300 pounds continuous tractive effort and up to 7,000 horsepower. Although very powerful, it is relatively short, measuring just 51 feet, 5.75 inches long.

Amtrak initially ordered 47 AEM-7s, delivered in the early 1980s. This allowed Amtrak to retire the last of its GG1 fleet in 1981 and to reassign the Pennsylvania Railroad-era *Metroliner* multiple units (MUs) to

A brand-new Amtrak HHP8 rests in the yard at Philadelphia's 30th Street Station in May 1999. These powerful locomotives use the same propulsion technology as the *Acela Express* trainsets and feature similar streamlining. Not be confused with *Acela Express* power cars, these are true locomotives and not semi-permanently coupled with a trainset. They are quickly identified because they have cabs at both ends. Because they are more powerful than the older AEM-7s, Amtrak often assigns the HHP-8s to long consists. *Richard Jay Solomon*

other duties. Amtrak ordered additional AEM-7s to replace locomotives damaged in accidents.

Single AEM-7s have generally been limited to hauling just 8 to 10 Amfleet cars, not because of propulsion limitations, but because of the practical limitations of its ability to provide HEP reliably to longer consists.

With the completion of the electrification to Boston, some of Amtrak's AEM-7s have been modernized with a three-phase AC-traction system similar to that used by the *Acela Express* HSTs. These upgraded locomotives are designated AEM-7AC. In 2004, Amtrak had 52 AEM-7 and AEM-7ACs on its active roster, of which 35 to 39 were needed to cover daily assignments.

High-Horsepower Locomotive

As of mid-2004, Amtrak's most recent electrics were 15 "high-horsepower locomotives" that carry Amtrak's model designation HHP-8 and were built by the Bombardier Alstom Consortium between 1999 and 2001. These double-ended, dual-cab locomotives use the same propulsion technology and similar styling as the *Acela Express* HST (see Chapter 5), and are numbered from 650 to 664. They have a continuous horsepower rating of 8,046 and a maximum intended speed of 135 miles per hour using a 71:23 gear ratio. These four-axle machines are 67 feet, 1 inch long and weigh 222,000 pounds. The HHP-8s are typically assigned to very long Amfleet NEC consists and long-distance trains that use the NEC, such as the *Silver Star* and *Silver Meteor*.

A pair of AEM-7ACs rests at the New Haven, Connecticut, Motor Storage on March 16, 2003. Since the extension of electrification to Boston in the year 2000, the need for Amtrak trains to change engines at New Haven is greatly reduced. However, some trains, such as the *Vermonter*, which use the line northward to Springfield, Massachusetts, still require a change. *Otto M. Vondrak*

Empire Corridor trains catch the morning sun as they lay over between runs at Niagara Falls, New York, in April 1989. Amfleet cars measure 85 feet, 4 inches long; 10 feet, 6 inches wide; and 12 feet, 8 inches tall. This profile allows them to operate without restriction on virtually all standard gauge railway routes in North America. *Brian Solomon*

CHAPTER FOUR

PASSENGER CARS

Amfleet

When Amtrak began service, it selected the best passenger cars from the railroads from whom it had assumed passenger operations. However, these cars were largely 20 to 30 years old and had been built to differing specifications by various manufacturers according to the needs of their original owners. Thus, there were a variety of compatibility problems and other operational headaches. In order to provide better service, Amtrak needed to buy new passenger cars for its intercity

The westward *Southwest Limited* reached Kansas City, Missouri, very early in the morning. At the time of this June 11, 1977, photograph, just three daily trains served Kansas City Union Station. In 1946, 128 daily trains had served the station. The full-length Superdome was one of several built by Pullman-Standard for the Milwaukee Road in 1952. Amtrak bought four from Milwaukee Road in 1972 and assigned them as lounges. Although popular with passengers, domes are expensive to maintain. *John Gruber*

operations. Amtrak decided upon a modern design patterned after the Budd-built Metroliner electric multiple unit cars. Paul Reistrup explained in the January 1981 *TRAINS* magazine that the new car design was initially known as the "Metro-Shell" until Amtrak hired the advertising firm Needham, Harper & Steers, which came up with the Amfleet moniker. Individual car configurations in this line were named Amcoach, Amcafe, Amclub, and Amdinette.

Amfleet cars differed from traditional passenger units in several key areas. Instead of using straight sides, the cars used a tubular design with curved sides like the Metroliner cars, which gave them a noticeably different profile. Tubular design and welded stainless steel made Amfleet cars exceptionally strong, capable of withstanding high-speed crashes with minimal car damage.

With Amfleet, Amtrak abandoned traditional steam heat and adopted the Head End Power (HEP) system, which relied on the locomotive to generate three-phase AC electrical power to provide on-board heating and lighting. Transformers on the cars step the voltage down for specific applications. Overhead fluorescent lights operate using 220-volt single-phase alternating current, while incandescent lights above seats and elsewhere in the cars work from

Amfleet has been the staple passenger car type on the Northeast Corridor since the mid-1970s. They use a simple, solid design that is safe and reliable and provides good ride quality. An AEM-7 leads a train consisting of Amfleet cars bound for New York City and Washington, D.C., near Fairfield, Connecticut, at 4:22 p.m. on March 5, 1987. *Brian Solomon*

120-volt single-phase alternating current. Although HEP had been used on commuter rail equipment since the late 1950s and on experimental long-distance trains such as the TurboTrains and Metroliners, it was a radical divergence from conventional practice to purchase a fleet of long-distance passenger cars with HEP. This meant that Amfleet cars would be incompatible with existing cars, unless provision was made to deliver both steam heat and HEP to the same train. Since Amfleet was initially bought for medium-distance corridor services, incompatibility was not expected to be a serious problem. The success of HEP on Amfleet cars on long-distance services, combined with difficulties using steam-heated equipment, ultimately led Amtrak to either convert or retire all inherited steam-heated cars. Amtrak's last steam-heated train operated in spring 1982.

Amfleet cars have a variety of other novel features, some of which are a function of modern travel. The windows are deliberately made smaller than on traditional cars as a response to vandalism, especially where stone throwing is a problem. The cars are designed for high-speed (120 miles per hour) operation and equipped with disc brakes incorporated in an unusual-looking truck that leaves the outer wheel surface exposed. Wheels have a 36-inch diameter, and an air-suspension system provides a smoother and quieter ride. Another result of high-speed service was the exclusive use of

An interior view of an Amdinette in service on train No. 86 (Richmond, Virginia-Boston) shows the dinette portion of the car with seats for 32 people. Typically, dinette seats are reserved for café customers and not for seat revenue. Amdinettes are considered food-service cars rather than full-service dining cars. Passengers can order snacks and drinks. *Brian Solomon*

Lead service attendant Tasha Knight works in an Amcafe on train No. 80, the Charlotte-New York City *Carolinian*. Amtrak passengers can enjoy a good selection of drinks, light meals, and snacks. Many trains carry regional brands in addition to major brand products. *Brian Solomon*

self-contained chemical toilets, nearly two decades before sanitary concerns resulted in a national mandate for self-contained toilets. The cars feature electrically operated doors, both to the outside and between the cars. Interior doors are opened using large rectangular push-button switches at both hand and foot level. While the electrically operated doors were a sound concept, they have been the source of chronic problems. Repeated kicking of the foot-level plates routinely results in failure, and water often shorts out these low-level switches.

Amtrak retired much of the HEP Heritage Fleet in the mid-1990s. The *Lake Shore Limited*, train No. 48, was photographed near Chicago on January 2, 1995 with Amtrak sleeper 2080 *Loch Sloy* and Amtrak's dome coach 9406. Dome coach 9406, was built in 1954 as Burlington 558, a pool service dome coach for Northern Pacific's flagship *North Coast Limited*, a train that traversed the Burlington between the Twin Cities and Chicago. Prior to rebuilding with HEP in 1983, the car carried the number 9485. *Brian Solomon*

Amfleet cars also feature an electrical public-address system for on-board announcements and music.

Amfleet cars were first ordered in October 1973, when Amtrak experienced a surge in ridership as a result of the Middle East oil embargo. They were built by Budd, representing from some 30 years of cumulative design experience in the construction of welded, stainless steel, streamlined passenger cars (one of Budd's first trains was Burlington's famous *Zephyr* of 1934). Amtrak placed four

This detail of Heritage Fleet sleeping car *Loch Katrine* was photographed in Chicago on March 4, 1995. This was a SlumberCoach built by Budd for Northern Pacific. *Brian Solomon*

orders for the original Amfleet cars, totaling 492 units, the last delivered in June 1977. The cars vary in weight depending on configuration, but typically weigh about 50 tons.

As built, conventional Amcoaches feature 84 seats per car, while cars built especially for long-distance trains have 60 seats, leaving more legroom and additional space for restrooms. Amcafes feature a central snack bar and room for 53 seats, while Amclubs have a central snack bar with 23 coach seats on one end of the car and 18 club seats on the other end. Amdinettes have a central snack bar, with 32 table seats at one end and 23 coach seats at the other.

Amfleet cars originally featured an interior decor in line with the aesthetic trends of the mid-1970s: dark browns, purples, orange, and deep reds were predominant. Some cars retained this styling, while others were redecorated during rebuilding in the 1990s and now feature brighter colors. Amfleet has proven to be a rugged and worthy design. The nearly 500 cars have served as the backbone of Amtrak's corridor services for nearly three decades, making them older now than were many of the heritage cars when Amtrak began.

Heritage Fleet

Amtrak's unfortunate experiences during the winter of 1976 and 1977 convinced it that HEP was the way of the future. Although not part of its original plan, Amtrak began converting some of its inherited steam-heated cars to HEP. Most of the work was accomplished at its Beech Grove Shops near Indianapolis in the late 1970s and early 1980s. A variety of cars, including standard 10-6 sleepers (10 "roomettes" and 6 double bedrooms), coaches, lounge-diners, and dome cars were eventually converted. Many cars received substantial refurbishing in addition to HEP equipment.

Conversion made the older cars compatible with new Amfleet cars. However, many of the most distinctive equipment, such as round-end observation cars, were not converted. By the year 2000, only a handful of heritage cars remained in service, mostly diners, baggage cars, and a few old sleepers used as crew dormitories on eastern long-distance trains.

Amfleet II

The success of the original Amfleet inspired Amtrak to return to Budd in 1980 for more low-level passenger cars of the same essential design, but incorporating a variety of minor improvements. In 1981, Budd delivered 150 new cars: 125 Amfleet II coaches and 25 Amlounges. Among the improvements were fewer external components, larger windows, and fewer seats per car. Amfleet II was intended for long-distance services and generally feature just 59 seats per car, with some cars having only 55 seats to allow more storage space. Amlounges feature a snack bar at one end, 17 lounge seats, and 32 table seats. Amfleet II cars have vestibules and external doors at just one end of the car, as opposed to both ends, as on the original Amfleet. These cars were typically assigned to eastern long-distance trains where passengers were expected to ride for more than just a few hours.

Superliners

When money for new cars was made available in the mid-1970s, Amtrak planned to acquire a fleet of deluxe bi-level cars for its western long-distance services, based largely on Santa Fe's successful bi-level *El Capitan* cars of 1956. The advantage of bi-levels is that each car has greater capacity and allows better views of western vistas. While Budd had built the old Santa Fe cars, Amtrak awarded the order for new bi-levels, known as Superliners, to Pullman-Standard. Amtrak placed its initial order on April 2, 1975, for 235 cars, which was eventually increased to a total of 284 at a cost of $241 million.

The first cars were originally expected in 1977 but were delayed because of a strike at Pullman. The first Superliner was finally delivered at the end of October 1978, and

At sunrise on October 25, 1993, train 30, the *Capitol Limited*, rolls east toward its station stop at Cumberland, Maryland, on the old Baltimore & Ohio. The *Capitol Limited* was one of the few Amtrak trains in the east to regularly carry a dome car. Riding over the B&O in a dome was one of the great Amtrak experiences. The dome allowed passengers to watch the train snake through the curves as it crossed the legendary Sand Patch grade in the Alleghenies. *Brian Solomon*

the cars made their initial debut in Chicago-Milwaukee service on February 26, 1979. Since the coaches were delivered first, Superliners were initially used in short-haul services in the Midwest and Pacific Northwest. On October 28, 1979—a year to the day after the first car was delivered—Amtrak's first Superliner-equipped long-distance train, No. 7, the westbound *Empire Builder,* departed Chicago for Seattle.

The last Pullman Superliner was a sleeping car completed at the end of July 1981. This

The *California Zephyr* descends the eastern slope of Donner Pass through the Truckee River Canyon on June 18, 1994. From left to right are a Superliner sleeper, two Superliner coaches, and a Superliner Sightseer café-lounge. Introduction of Superliners in the late 1970s and early 1980s ended the use of traditional, steam-heated streamlined cars on western long-distance routes. The colorful era that had mixed and matched a variety of heritage equipment gave way to relative uniformity. *Brian Solomon*

final car was also the very last built by Pullman, a firm that had been synonymous with sleeping cars for over a century. The last car was named in honor of the company's founder, George Mortimer Pullman. With its completion, an era in passenger car-building had come to a close.

Superliners are 85 feet long; 10 feet, 2 inches wide; and 16 feet, 2 inches tall. The car's height, 3½ feet taller than Amfleet, has restricted their operation on many low-clearance lines, especially in the east. The typical car weighs about 157,000 pounds, but instead of the end vestibules that are typical of most North American passenger cars, Superliners use centrally located doors for boarding. The interior of the cars is spacious, and coach seating was based on first-class airline standards, which give passengers plenty of legroom. Full Superliner coaches were built with 75 seats. In addition to coaches there are Superliner sleepers with 15 economy bedrooms, 5 deluxe bedrooms,

Superliner coach/baggage 31035 heads toward Chicago Union Station via the former Alton Route at the multiple crossing in Brighton Park comprising the old Pennsylvania Railroad Panhandle, Baltimore & Ohio Chicago Terminal, and former New York Central Chicago Junction. The 85-foot-long Superliner straddles the entire crossing. *Brian Solomon*

Superliner II cars were built in Vermont by Bombardier and delivered to Amtrak in 1994. This close-up shows the side of Superliner II sleeper *Connecticut*. Ironically, this car cannot operate in the state it was named for because it is too tall to conform to Amtrak clearances there. *Brian Solomon*

a family-sized bedroom, and a handicapped bedroom. There are also diners with seats for 72; coach-baggage cars; and café-lounges, known colloquially as "sightseer lounges," which feature a glass roof for taking in western panoramas. A number of Superliners have been reconfigured into new arrangements since the 1980s.

The old Santa Fe bi-levels were often used in conjunction with Superliners and could be easily spotted by their slightly lower profile and distinct side-fluting pattern. In some cases, the Santa Fe cars were used in a step-up capacity to allow movement between single-level and Superliner cars.

By the late 1980s, many eastern railroads had raised clearances to allow for the movement of tri-level covered auto-carriers and double-stack container trains. Although unintended, this also allowed for the use of Superliners east of Chicago.

In the early 1990s, Amtrak ordered 140 Superliner IIs from Canadian manufacturer Bombardier, which constructed the cars at its Barre, Vermont, facility. Amtrak paid $340 million for these cars, and their delivery in 1993 allowed for the expanded use of bi-level equipment on some eastern runs—both *Capitol Limited* (trains 30 and 31) and *AutoTrain* were converted to Superliner operation in the mid-1990s.

Horizon Cars

By the late 1980s, all the traditional American passenger car manufacturers had exited the market and commuter agencies had largely turned to Canadian manufacturer Bombardier. Bombardier had acquired both Budd and Pullman-Standard passenger car patents, so in 1988, when Amtrak had a demand for new single-level medium-distance cars, it ordered 104 units from Bombardier: 86 coaches and 18 food-service cars. These were essentially adapted from a commuter rail design derived from Pullman patents and closely resemble commuter cars delivered to NJ Transit, Metro-North (New York), and MBTA (Boston). They feature brushed-aluminum bodies with straight sides and very small rectangular windows. They cost slightly less than $1 million apiece and are known on Amtrak as the Horizon Fleet. Horizon Cars were built at Bombardier's Barre, Vermont, plant and delivered during 1988 and 1989.

Viewliners

Development of a new line of low-level passenger equipment for service on Amtrak's eastern routes began in 1981 during the Alan Boyd regime, but the better part of 15 years passed before the first production cars entered revenue service. Unlike the high-level Superliners, which can only operate on lines with tall clearances, the Viewliners were intended for operation on all Amtrak routes. According to *Passenger Train Journal,* Amtrak developed the Viewliner using Budd's stainless steel designs. Three prototype cars, one diner and two sleepers, were assembled at Amtrak's

Beech Grove Shops in 1987 and 1988. The sleepers were originally numbered 2300 and 2301 and entered service on the *Auto Train* in early 1988.

Amtrak needed Viewliners to replace worn-out Heritage Fleet cars, many of which had seen more than 40 years of hard service. Although the Viewliner has become Amtrak's sole eastern-route sleeping car, *TRAINS* reported that initially Amtrak planned to buy dining cars, lounges, and baggage/crew dorms as part of the fleet. These other types were scuttled as a result of continuing financial crisis in the early 1990s.

After more than four years of testing and more than a decade of discussion and planning, on December 2, 1992, Amtrak's board of directors authorized Morrison-Knudsen (M-K) to construct 50 Viewliner sleepers. Financial difficulties at both Amtrak and M-K further delayed manufacture. In 1995 and 1996, the

After a day of watching freight trains cross Stevens Pass in the Cascade Mountains, Jack Whitley enjoys the passing of Amtrak's eastbound *Empire Builder* while relaxing on a trackside bench in Skykomish, Washington, on September 14, 2002. The Superliner II sleeper *Oklahoma* pictured here was part of an order for 140 bi-levels built by Canadian car-builder Bombardier. *Tom Kline*

The collapse of Penn Central created opportunity for Amtrak. Among the facilities Amtrak purchased from PC were the former Pennsylvania Railroad's 14th Street Coach Yards in Chicago. In the late 1970s, Amtrak transformed this facility into a modern yard that is today responsible for servicing hundreds of cars that work Chicago trains daily. This midnight view from the control tower shows the expanse of the yards against the backdrop of Chicago's famous Sears Tower. *Brian Solomon*

order was completed by M-K's railcar-building successor, American Passenger Rail Car Company (Amerail). Assembly was done at the former Erie Railroad shops in Hornell, New York.

There were some relatively minor design changes between the prototypes and production cars. Based on Amtrak specifications, Viewliner sleeper dimensions are 85

feet, 4 inches long; 10 feet, 6 inches wide; and 14 feet tall; and they weigh 140,500 pounds. Production cars cost about $2 million apiece, and each features 12 standard bedrooms, six on each side of the car, two deluxe bedrooms, and one handicapped bedroom. The standard bedrooms, designed for two people, are 79 inches long, 83 inches wide, and 102 inches high. They feature two facing seats with a retractable table between them. The seats can be transformed into a lower bunk, while the upper bunk can be lowered into place. The upper row of windows allows a view from the top bunk. Sink and non-enclosed toilet facilities are included in the Standard bedroom. Additional toilet facilities are located down the corridor. Although small, the Standard bedroom is a pleasant and comfortable travel space. It offers privacy and amenities above and beyond railroad coach travel, and is remarkably better than economy sleeping car accommodation provided by most European railways. Viewliner Deluxe bedrooms are substantially larger and designed for larger groups of people. These also feature enclosed toilet and shower facilities.

Viewliners are repaired and maintained at Beech Grove Shops and at Amtrak's Hialeah, Florida, facility. Production cars are numbered from 62000 to 62049, and each carries a name

On February 20, 2004, Amtrak No. 90, the northward *Palmetto* (Miami–New York City) accelerates away from its station stop at Dillon, South Carolina. Amfleet II cars, as seen on No. 90, feature slightly larger windows and vestibules at only one end. The cars were designed for long-distance services and with just 55 to 59 seats per car, afford more legroom than 84-seat corridor-service Amfleet cars. *Brian Solomon*

ending in "View," with 62000 designated *American View*. They have been typically assigned to eastern long-distance trains that operate on routes, which cannot accommodate Superliner equipment. These include New York-Florida trains, Boston and New York sections of the *Lake Shore Limited*, New York City–Chicago *Three Rivers*, New York City–Washington, D.C.–Chicago *Cardinal*, New York City–New Orleans *Crescent*, and as of this writing, seasonally on the Boston–Washington, D.C., overnight train known as the *Federal*.

The Viewliner has allowed Amtrak to continue to offer quality sleeping car service between major eastern cities. Passengers can enjoy waking up with views of Pennsylvania's Juniata Valley, the shores of Lake Erie, and the Connecticut shoreline. Arriving by sleeping car remains a first-class experience and one of the great pleasures of modern American railway travel.

Although pleasing and comfortable from a passenger's perspective, the Viewliner design suffers from several shortcomings that have resulted in relatively poor car availability. Many of the components are special designs and cannot be obtained cheaply or readily. In some cases, they need to be custom-made just for Amtrak. As a result it can take weeks or months to fix sidelined cars. In addition to the three prototypes stored at Beech Grove, in early 2004 approximately 20 unserviceable Viewliners were awaiting repairs. As a result, it is not unusual for some trains normally scheduled to carry sleepers to run without them.

California Cars

To provide equipment for state-supported services, the California Department of Transportation (California DOT) ordered 88 double-deck, push-pull passenger cars from Morrison-Knudsen in February 1992 for

delivery in 1994. The order was later reduced to 66 cars. M-K was reorganized during production, and Amerail completed the order.

The cars' styling and profile matches that of the Amtrak F59PHI diesels bought to propel them. The locomotives supply 480-volt, three-phase HEP. Although often operated in matched sets, the California Cars were designed to work in conjunction with other Amtrak equipment. The cars are 85 feet long (over coupler faces); 10 feet, 2.5 inches wide; and 16 feet, 1.5 inches tall. The order included 14 cab cars (with a control cab for push mode) numbered in the 8300 series. These weigh 155,000 pounds each and have seats for 86 passengers. Thirty-two standard trailer coaches were ordered, numbered in the 8000 series, weighing 151,000 pounds with seats for 90 passengers. There are also six coach/baggage trailers numbered in the 8200 series, weighing 151,000 pounds with seats for

84 passengers. When the cars are fully loaded with passengers, they weigh an estimated 190,000 pounds. In addition, there are 14 food-service cars numbered in the 8800 series. The majority of seats are located on the upper level. Cab cars have the control compartment on the upper level and are equipped with headlights, warning lights, marker lights, and horns. The engineer's controls are similar to those used on the F59PHI locomotives.

Between 2000 and 2002, more double-deck cars were bought by Amtrak and California DOT for use in *Pacific Surfliner* service (San Diego–Los Angeles–San Luis Obispo) and other California Amtrak services. This order consisted of nine five-car sets built in Hornell, New York, by Alstom. Amtrak funded eight sets, California another. In their original configuration, each set consists of a business-class car (numbered in the 6800 series), two coaches (6400 series), a coach/café

The Viewliner is Amtrak's modern single-level sleeping car. On July 18, 1997, the *Wayside View* car 62048 works the *Twilight Shoreliner* from Newport News, Virginia, to Boston. *Brian Solomon*

An interior view North Carolina DOT's coach *Honey Bee* used for Amtrak's Raleigh-Charlotte *Piedmont*, trains 73 and 74. Pullman-Standard built this car for Kansas City Southern in 1965. It was one of five such cars acquired by North Carolina DOT and refurbished by the Delaware Car Company between 1992 and 1995. Each car is named to honor state flora and fauna and is decorated with state symbols. The honeybee is North Carolina's state insect. *Brian Solomon*

(6300 series), and a cab car with coach and baggage space (6900 series). Additional F59PHIs were bought for expanded Amtrak West services, some of which were specially painted to match the liveries of the *Pacific Surfliner* cars.

TALGO

Amtrak has experimented with TALGO low-profile articulated pendular trains since 1988, when it imported a *Talgo Prototipo de Alta Velocidad* from Spain for testing on the Northeast Corridor. Despite successful testing the train was returned. TALGO passenger car

On March 11, 1999, F59PHI 2003 leads train 711 (Bakersfield–Oakland), the *San Joaquin*, at Pinole, California. The train consists of four bi-level California Cars that were paid for by the state for use on corridor services. The *San Joaquin* began in 1974 with a single daily roundtrip. Today, there are five daily Oakland–Bakersfield trains, plus a daily Sacramento-Bakersfield roundtrip. *Brian Jennison*

bodies use an unconventional lightweight tubular design and are coupled together in fixed articulated sets that straddle a common set of wheels. Instead of trucks, TALGO uses specially designed wheel pairs in which the wheels are independent of each other rather than coupled to a common axle to reduce wheel wear and permit a low-profile, low-center-of-gravity train capable of relatively high speeds. Various types of TALGO trains have served the Spanish national railway, RENFE, since the 1950s. Early, non-pendular, TALGOs were also used in the United States by Boston & Maine, New Haven, and Rock Island.

In 1994, Amtrak's renewed interest in TALGO resulted in the importation of a 12-car TP-200 consist for experimental service between Seattle and Portland. Service with this train was expanded in 1995 to work between Eugene, Oregon, and Vancouver, British Columbia. In 1995, a 14-car TP-200 train-set was imported for a nationwide demonstration tour, and ultimately this train was also assigned to service in the Pacific Northwest.

According to the November 2001 *Today's Railways*, Washington State's interest in three TP-200 trains (one purchased by Amtrak, the other two by Washington) to expand services in the Pacific Northwest led to the creation of an American subsidiary called Talgo America, Inc., to provide maintenance, assembly, and support of the unusual trains. These trains were delivered in 1998 and began *Cascades* service between Eugene, Oregon, Seattle, and Vancouver, British Columbia, in 1999. They feature a specialized exterior design, complete with fiberglass fins to make for a more uniform transition between F59PHI diesels and the low-slung trains. They are operated with non-powered control units at one end for push-pull operation. The trains are painted in a distinctive cream, brown, and dark-green livery that reflects the image of the Pacific Northwest.

Cascades service in the Pacific Northwest uses Spanish TALGO TP-200 pendular trains. Trains are normally run as push-pull consists with an EMD F59PHI locomotive at one end and a non-powered control unit (NPCU) rebuilt from an EMD F40PH at the other. On July 7, 2001, F59PHI leads a TP-200 working as train 507, the midday departure from Seattle to Eugene, Oregon, a few miles from its terminus. *Brian Jennison*

Amtrak's Washington, D.C.-Boston *Acela Express* glides along the Northeast Corridor (NEC) at Westport, Connecticut. This section of the NEC is owned and operated by Metro-North. Due to a combination of numerous curves and very heavy Metro-North commuter traffic, Amtrak trains cannot operate at maximum speeds on Metro-North's line. *Brian Solomon*

CHAPTER FIVE

SELF-PROPELLED TRAINS

United Aircraft TurboTrain

In the 1930s, Americans developed a fascination for sexy and lightweight streamlined articulated passenger trains. The articulated streamliners of the 1930s resulted in the development of conventionally run streamlined passenger cars that largely replaced traditional heavyweight passenger cars during the 1940s and 1950s. These cars captured the essence of the

early streamliners while using proven and more practical technology. The next wave of lightweight articulated trains came in the 1950s and included Electro-Motive's *Aero Train*, Boston & Maine's and New Haven's imported TALGOs, and Chesapeake & Ohio's (C&O) *Train-X*. However, all were complete failures and most only operated for a few years.

The High Speed Ground Transportation Act of 1965, which made federal funds available to promote the development of high-speed trains (HSTs), resulted in another generation of lightweight train designs. A new spin was put on the lightweight articulated train in the form of gas-turbine propulsion.

Gas turbines were not new to railroading. During the previous decade, Union Pacific had bought GE gas turbine–electrics for heavy long-distance freight service. Yet, the practical application of turbine power in high-speed passenger service was a novel concept.

United Aircraft (UA) developed the TurboTrain, an articulated aerodynamic passenger train with pendular suspension powered by five, Pratt & Whitney, 400-horsepower ST-6B gas turbines that powered the wheels through direct gear drive. Its pendular suspension minimized the effects of centrifugal forces on passengers on curves at high speed. UA had acquired C&O's *Train-X* patents and according to Michael P. Chaney in *Railroad History Bulletin 154*, the TurboTrain's pendular suspension system was derived from *Train-X*.

TurboTrain was designed in a wind tunnel and like contemporary aircraft was entirely constructed of welded aluminum. In the

March 1970 *TRAINS*, William D. Middleton noted the train weighed just half that of diesel-hauled passenger equipment. The combination of its wind-resistant design, guided axles to reduce wheel-rail resistance in curves, and high-powered turbines allowed for very fast running. Middleton said that TurboTrain could operate through curves at an estimated 36 to 46 percent faster than conventional equipment.

TurboTrain was intended to provide a faster, more comfortable service on existing tracks than was possible with conventional train design. The hope was that the TurboTrain could be used to provide high-speed train service without the need for intensive and expensive mainline infrastructure improvements normally required for fast service.

TurboTrain was a shortcut to high-speed service without the need to rebuild, relocate, or electrify mainlines.

Assembled by Pullman-Standard in Chicago, TurboTrain debuted in May 1967, and in November 1967, a TurboTrain tested at 170.8 miles per hour on the Pennsylvania Railroad's long tangent between New Brunswick and Trenton, New Jersey. It was hoped that TurboTrain would allow the railroads to effectively compete with the airlines in short intercity corridors. Penn Central placed the TurboTrain in Boston-Grand Central revenue service on April 8, 1969, although top speed was limited to 100 miles per hour because of the track and signaling conditions on the route. By June 1969, the Boston-New York City run was

A five-car United Aircraft TurboTrain working as train 151, the *Flying Yankee*, departs New Haven, Connecticut, on February 12, 1976. Amtrak had expanded the TurboTrains from three to five cars. Despite this increase in capacity, they were deemed unsuccessful and Amtrak withdrew them from regular service in September 1976 when new EMD F40PH diesels and Budd-built Amfleet passenger cars arrived. *George Kowanski*

The RTG Turboliners built by ANF-Frengeco had a decidedly European appearance. Externally, they were nearly the same as turbos operated by French National Railways (SNCF). In August 1977, an RTG Turboliner negotiates the double slip switches at Chicago Union Station. This is train No. 364, the *Blue Water Limited*, bound for Port Huron, Michigan. Slip switches use multiple sets of points, combining the function of a switch and a crossing. *Steve Smedley*

made in 3 hours and 39 minutes. On the eve of Amtrak's debut, the service was rerouted to New York's Penn Station so TurboTrain could connect with Metroliner electric services to Washington, D.C.

Amtrak inherited TurboTrain and the prerogative to operate high-speed rail service in the Northeast in May 1971. TurboTrain's sleek modern appearance was exactly the image Amtrak hoped to promote, and it was featured in advertisements, timetables, and brochures. Early in Amtrak's life, TurboTrain toured the United States in fresh Amtrak paint, visiting some 31 states.

In 1972, Amtrak expanded its three UA TurboTrains from three to five cars. For the rest of their tenure on Amtrak, they primarily worked between Boston and Penn Station. In general, the trains were popular with passengers, who enjoyed the views from the elevated domes at the front and rear. However, on jointed rail the ride could be rough. Clark Johnson Jr., who rode the trains on several

occasions, remarked, "They were very loud, much more so than a conventional train." George Kowanski, an engineer who ran TurboTrains said, "Everything about them was like an aircraft except the throttle, which resembled that used on a trolley car."

Despite its promise, the UA TurboTrain suffered from a variety of problems that were common with earlier lightweight train designs. Its inflexible consist, poor ride-quality on rough track, and high maintenance costs made operations expensive. Chaney also explained, "While [the TurboTrain had] a 160-mph potential, the railroad lines did not."

Withdrawn in 1976, the TurboTrains were stored for several years before being scrapped in the early 1980s. Amtrak eventually achieved relatively high-speed running on the Boston–New York City route through infrastructure improvements, electrification, and the use of the *Acela Express* electric tilting train-sets. Canadian National (and later VIA Rail) also operated a fleet of UA TurboTrains,

which had a better success record and survived in revenue service until 1982.

RTG Turboliners

Amtrak was desperate for new equipment in its formative years. In 1972, it ordered two five-car RTG turbo-powered trains from French manufacturer ANF (according to the January 1988 *CTC Board*, RTG stands for Ram Turbine Gas). These were of a stock design used by the French National Railways adapted for North American service and delivered in October 1973. Like the UA TurboTrain, the RTGs had a power car at each end, an arrangement that simplifies reversing at terminal stations. Turbomeca Tumo III gas turbines were used to power driving wheels using a Voith torque converter (hydraulic transmission). Each turbine generated 1,140 horsepower.

The ANF-RTG turbos were assigned to Chicago and initially worked the Chicago–St. Louis route. Pleased with these trains, Amtrak

ordered four more RTGs that were delivered in 1975 and also assigned to Chicago, where they were maintained at a specialized shop at Brighton Park. Their last regular assignment was on the Chicago–Milwaukee corridor, a relatively high-speed run where Milwaukee Road's famous *Hiawatha*s once raced along at speeds in excess of 100 miles per hour behind Atlantic- and Hudson-type steam locomotives. In 1981, the RTG turbos were withdrawn from Midwest service and placed in long-term storage.

Empire Corridor Turboliners

Amtrak's experience with its RTG turbo sets led it to order seven more similar trains manufactured domestically under license by Rohr Industries at Chula Vista, California. (Rohr had also built subway cars for the Bay Area Rapid Transit, and Washington, D.C., Metro systems.) These were delivered during 1976 and 1977. According to *Railway Gazette International*, these were originally ordered

Following rebuilding, the RTG Turboliners closely resembled the Rohr turbos. An Amtrak RTG-II set zips along the Hudson River near Peekskill, New York, on its run from Albany-Rensselaer to Grand Central in August 1989. *Brian Solomon*

A brand-new Rohr Turboliner working the *Adirondack* (Montreal–New York City) pauses for a station stop at Fort Edward, New York, on the Delaware & Hudson. *Jim Shaughnessy*

A Rohr Turboliner zips along the Hudson Valley at Breakneck Ridge near Cold Spring, New York, in the fading light of a late-summer evening in 1989. Rohr trains were equipped with third-rail shoes and traction motors for operation in New York–area third-rail territory. *Brian Solomon*

for Boston-New York service. Change in Amtrak's NEC operating strategy, however, resulted in the Rohr trains being assigned to New York's Empire Corridor services (a separate fleet of Rohr trains had been considered for this route).

The basic configuration and technology of the RTG and Rohr trains are the same. However, the Rohr trains exhibited several significant improvements. According to El Simon in the July 1996 *Passenger Train Journal*, the Rohr trains had been redesigned to better suit the rigors of American railroad operations. Instead of employing a European coupler, they used a knuckle coupler to allow Turboliner cars to be hauled by conventional equipment. While not used in regular passenger service,

this feature aided in the movement of cars to and from shops. Rohr cabs featured a different profile designed to enhance forward visibility and improve crash protection. Where the RTG turbos featured European-style bulbous ends, the Rohr turbos featured a distinctive and more angular shovel-nose profile.

For two decades these train-sets operated the majority of New York-Albany services, whisking passengers along the Hudson River at speeds up to 110 miles per hour. The trains' large windows were popular with passengers who enjoyed the splendid Hudson Valley scenery. The trains also worked along the former New York Central Water Level Route to Buffalo and Niagara Falls, as well as on the *Adirondack* to Montreal.

Empire Corridor Turboliners are maintained at Amtrak's Rensselaer Shops adjacent to the Albany-Rensselaer passenger station on the east bank of the Hudson. Amtrak RTG-II turbo powercar No. 66 reflects the sunset on December 2, 1990, at Rensselaer, New York. Chicago-based RTG turbos were maintained at Brighton Park. *Jim Shaughnessy*

Amtrak boosted its Empire service turbo fleet in 1987 when it rebuilt three stored RTG turbos for New York service. These trains were redesignated RTG-II, and new nose sections were fabricated to match the profile of the Rohr sets. The six power cars were numbered 64 to 69. These trains were not as successful as the Rohr turbos. According to *Passenger Train Journal,* in 1994 car No. 64 was involved in a self-consuming fire at New York's Penn Station resulting in the withdrawal of RTG-IIs.

Modern Empire Corridor Turbos

New York State has retained its fascination with the Rohr turbo trains. In the late 1990s, New York and Amtrak initially agreed to have the seven Rohr sets rebuilt and modernized for fast service on the Empire Corridor, with New York DOT financing the rebuilding. Initially, New York planned to boost top speeds to 125

miles per hour, but rebuilding suffered setbacks during the first years of the new millennia. Work was done at SuperSteel in Schenectady, New York, and by February 2004, three trains were available for revenue service. A total of four were expected for service based on the terms of a revised agreement. According to SuperSteel, the rebuilding includes structural remanufacturing, improvements to the traction system, a redesigned interior, improved vestibules, and better engine airflow. This unique Turboliner fleet offers the only opportunity passengers have to ride gas turbine–powered trains in North America. Today, they are some of the world's most unusual passenger trains.

Metroliners

Development of the Metroliner electric multiple-unit (MU) in the 1960s was a direct

response to the success of the Japanese Shinkansen. Using federal funding appropriated through the High Speed Ground Transportation Act, the Pennsylvania Railroad worked with Budd to develop high-speed electric MUs for its New York–Philadelphia–Washington, D.C., service. Budd built 61 stainless steel cars using a distinctive tubular design. These self-propelled cars drew power from PRR's 11,000-volt AC overhead catenary using transformers and rectifiers to supply direct current for traction motors. The original Metroliner cars entered service on Penn Central in 1969. In 1971, Amtrak inherited the cars, along with the mandate to operate the *Metroliner* service.

(Note: Metroliner equipment must be distinguished from *Metroliner* service. *Metroliner*, when italicized, refers to the high-speed train service [New York to Washington, D.C.]; when Metroliner is not italicized, it refers strictly to the cars. Not all *Metroliners* have used Metroliner cars, and Metroliner cars have not always worked as *Metroliners*.)

Metroliner service was popular, but the high-speed MUs were plagued with reliability problems and Amtrak contracted to have them rebuilt in the mid-1970s. After delivery of the AEM-7s in the early 1980s, Amtrak reassigned the Metroliner MUs to Philadelphia–Harrisburg *Keystone* services. The *Metroliner*-brand service was then operated using AEM-7s and Amfleet cars. In the mid-1980s, some of the MU cab-control cars were rebuilt for service on diesel-powered push-pull trains.

One of Amtrak's rebuilt Metroliner multiple units working in premier *Metroliner* service passes Hunter Tower in Newark, New Jersey, on October 21, 1983. Rebuilt Metroliners featured an extended hump on the roof for electrical equipment that was not part of the original design. *Doug Eisele*

A Budd SPV2000 lays over at Springfield, Massachusetts, between runs on a summer evening in 1985. These diesel rail cars often operated singly on the Springfield–Hartford–New Haven connecting service, but were not successful. Although diesel railcars are widely used for light passenger runs on many railways around the world, the concept has not appealed to modern North American railways. *Brian Solomon*

Diesel Railcars

Amtrak inherited a small fleet of Budd-built rail diesel cars, known in the industry as RDCs or Budd cars. Built in the 1950s, they were intended to allow railroads to reduce operating costs on lightly traveled routes and suburban lines. Budd built a total of 398 cars, of which Amtrak got just 24. Most of Amtrak's RDCs were former New Haven Railroad cars, including three experimental cars built in 1956 for New Haven's *Roger Williams* service. The end cars of this train featured streamlined cabs similar to those used on diesel-electric locomotives of the period.

Amtrak's RDCs were numbered from 10 to 43. They were typically assigned to the New Haven-Hartford-Springfield shuttles,

but were also used on the Chicago-Dubuque, Iowa, *Black Hawk*. Among the last two cars in service were Nos. 34 and 36, of New York Central and New Haven vintage, respectively. These were colloquially known in their last years as "The Duke and the Dutchess" because they were "old, stately, and almost always seen together." They survived on the Springfield run until 1986.

In 1978, Budd debuted its SPV-2000, which it hoped would be the successor to its original RDC. This self-propelled car used the Metro-shell body common to the Metroliner MUs and Amfleet. According to *Railway Gazette International*, the SPV-2000 was designed to meet the American Association of Railroad strength requirements. The

United Aircraft's (UA) TurboTrain pays a visit to Albany–Rensselaer. Later, this would become the maintenance base for Rohr and RTG-II Turboliners. The UA TurboTrain was mostly an unsuccessful attempt to apply aircraft technology to a state-of-the-art passenger train. *Jim Shaughnessy*

One of the Turboliners rebuilt by SuperSteel works New York City-Albany train No. 257 at Stockport on September 7, 2003. *Otto M. Vondrak*

at New Haven in order to offer through service to Springfield and Washington, D.C. This arrangement lasted only a few months.

Although SPV was supposed to stand for "self-propelled vehicle," the cars were notoriously unreliable and soon acquired the unfortunate nickname "seldom powered vehicles" among operators. They were withdrawn from Amtrak services by 1986 and replaced with reliable F40PH-hauled trains.

High-Speed Train: Acela Express

Amtrak's fastest scheduled service, the *Acela Express,* uses 20 specially designed high-speed train-sets, known to Amtrak as HSTs.

The *Acela Express* HSTs were built by a consortium of Bombardier and Alstom and assembled at Barre, Vermont, with some final work performed in New York State. Built between 1998 and 2000, the HSTs are of a unique design that blends the active tilting mechanism developed for Canada's Light Rapid Comfortable (LRC) trains during the 1970s and 1980s with French propulsion technology engineered for the Trains à Grande Vitesse (TGV). Only the passenger cars tilt, which is solely necessary for greater passenger comfort at higher speeds. Top speed in revenue service is 150 miles per hour.

One locomotive power car is located at each end of the train-set, each powered by state-of-the-art, three-phase propulsion system technology made possible by advances in semiconductor technology and microprocessor computer control. The *Acela Express* locomotives are multivoltage and draw power from the various voltages now used to energize different sections of the Northeast Corridor: 11 kV at 25 Hz, 13.2 kV at 60 Hz (nominal), and 25 kV at 60 Hz. The voltages are a function of the complex electrical histories of the different sections of the Northeast Corridor that remain to accommodate older existing suburban trains operating over the individual segments and because of the prohibitively high cost of converting the entire line to

In 1980, Amtrak experimented with a Bombardier-built LRC (Light-Rapid-Comfortable) train, testing it on the Northeast Corridor. This view shows the powercar at New Haven, Connecticut, in November 1980. Although the Canadian passenger operator VIA Rail bought these trains, they were not bought by Amtrak. The LRC tilting system was the basis for that used on the *Acela Express* HSTs. *J. J. Grumblatt Jr.*

prototype featured a futuristic streamlined nose section and was powered by a 360-horsepower General Motors Detroit Diesel engine. Budd hoped to sell hundreds of SPVs for use on runs under 200 miles. The Connecticut Department of Transportation purchased 13 of the cars under the direction of Elizabeth Leonard, and Amtrak operated them on the New Haven–Hartford–Springfield shuttle, and by Metro-North on its commuter branchline services to Waterbury and Danbury, Connecticut.

SPV-2000s featured a stainless steel body with side striping that matched Amtrak's Amfleet, with which they were designed to operate. This was to allow them to couple on the back of Boston–Washington, D.C., trains

the modern 25 kV at 60 Hz. Each locomotive can provide up to 6,169 continuous horsepower, giving the train a total of 12,338 horsepower. High horsepower is needed for rapid acceleration and to maintain continuous high speeds. Maximum designed speed is 165 miles per hour.

The HSTs have proven popular with passengers and have helped Amtrak secure a larger share of commercial passenger traffic in the Boston-New York-Washington, D.C., corridor. Unfortunately, the trains have suffered from a variety of technical problems. Early on, they made news when it was revealed that the cars were designed 4 inches too wide to take full advantage of the tilt mechanism. In the

event that two trains suffered simultaneous tilt failures while passing on a curve there was the potential for contact between trains. After the trains entered service, cracks in the wheel sets forced withdrawal of the entire fleet. The trains were made safe, but an interview with David Gunn published in December 2003/January 2004 *Mass Transit* magazine quoted his opinion of the trains:

> The passengers love the [train] but its performance has been woefully inadequate compared to the specifications in terms of failure rates. And none of them met specifications. We're having premature traction motor failures. We're having

Amtrak's rebuilt Metroliner blasts through Elizabeth, New Jersey, on July 26, 1980. Amtrak has retained the *Metroliner* service name, although locomotive-hauled trains are now used. Today, some of the old Metroliner cabcars are used as unpowered cab-control cars on push-pull trains.
J. J. Grumblatt Jr.

main suspension springs break. We're having dog bones on the tilt mechanism fracture and break.

Gunn elaborated on the decision-making process that led to the selection of the Bombardier/Alstom-designed HSTs, explaining that if you talk with Amtrak's operating people, they would agree that the Swedish X2000 was the train they should have bought. Gunn noted, "It was reliable, simple, proven" and "The reason we got into this mess is because the Canadian government is great at providing financing."

Perhaps if the U.S. government had supplied sufficient financing from the beginning Amtrak would not have had such difficulties. Ongoing technical problems have frustrated Amtrak and resulted in well-publicized

A recently rebuilt Turboliner whirs passed a riverside park at Stuyvesant, New York, on its daily journey between New York City and Albany–Rensselaer on April 6, 2004.
Brian Solomon

tension between the railroad and Bombardier and Alstom. In March 2004, Amtrak and the builders agreed to settle their disputes.

As of early 2004, Amtrak normally requires 14 HSTs for daily *Acela Express* services. In addition, two trains are held serviceable in standby, one at Washington, D.C., the other in Boston, in the event of train failure. Despite the problems, which normally do not affect the traveling public, riding the trains is a great thrill. They remain

Acela Express high-speed trains (HSTs) are permitted 150-mile-per-hour top speeds on specific upgraded sections of the Northeast Corridor (NEC) east of New London, Connecticut. Between New York City and Philadelphia, the trains reach 135 miles per hour on designated sections. Working under wires commissioned for revenue service in 2000, an *Acela Express* rolls toward New Haven in October 2002. *Brian Solomon*

Amtrak's premier service, and the combination of excellent interior design, great acceleration, and active tilting is one of the most interesting experiences in modern American railroading.

BIBLIOGRAPHY

Books

Allen, G. Freeman. *The Fastest Trains in the World.* London, 1978.

Anderson, Craig T. *Amtrak: The National Rail Passenger Corporation, 1978–1979 Annual.* San Francisco, Calif., 1978.

Armstrong, John H. *The Railroad: What It Is, What It Does.* Omaha, Neb., 1982.

Bradley, Rodger. *Amtrak: The US National Railroad Passenger Corporation.* Poole, Dorset, U.K., 1985.

Bush, Donald J. *The Streamlined Decade.* New York, 1975.

Centre Georges Pompidou. *All Stations: A Journey through 150 Years of Railway History.* Paris, 1978.

Churella, Albert J. *From Steam to Diesel.* Princeton, N.J., 1998.

Condit, Carl. *Port of New York, Vols. 1 & 2.* Chicago, 1980 and 1981.

Cupper, Dan. *Horseshoe Heritage: The Story of a Great Railroad Landmark.* Halifax, Pa., 1996.

Daughen, Joseph R., and Peter Binzen. *The Wreck of the Penn Central.* Boston, 1971.

Diehl, Lorraine B. *The Late Great Pennsylvania Station.* New York, 1985.

Doherty, Timothy Scott, and Brian Solomon. *Conrail.* St. Paul, Minn., 2004.

Dorin, Patrick. *Amtrak: Trains & Travel.* Seattle, Wash., 1979.

Droege, John A. *Passenger Terminals and Trains.* New York, 1916.

Drury, George H. *The Historical Guide to North American Railroads.* Waukesha, Wis., 1985.

Farrington Jr., S. Kip. *Railroading from the Rear End.* New York, 1946.

——.*Railroads at War.* New York, 1944.

——.*Railroads of Today.* New York, 1949.

Fischler, Stan. *Next Stop Grand Central.* Erin, Ont., Canada, 1986.

Frailey, Fred W. *Zephyrs, Chiefs & Other Orphans: The First Five Years of Amtrak.* Godfrey, Ill., 1977.

Harlow, Alvin F. *The Road of the Century.* New York, 1947.

——.*Steelways of New England.* New York, 1946.

Hollingsworth, Brian. *Modern Trains.* London, 1985.

Hollingsworth, Brian, and Arthur Cook. *Modern Locomotives.* London, 1983.

Jones, Robert W. *Boston & Albany: The New York Central in New England, Vols. 1 & 2.* Los Angeles, 1997.

Klein, Aaron E. *The History of the New York Central System.* New York, 1985.

Lyon, Peter. *To Hell in a Day Coach.* Philadelphia, Pa., 1968.

Marre, Louis A., and Jerry A. Pinkepank. *The Contemporary Diesel Spotter's Guide.* Milwaukee, Wis., 1985.

——.*Diesel Locomotives: The First 50 Years.* Waukesha, Wis., 1995.

Middleton, William D. *From Bullets to BART.* Chicago, 1989.

——.*Manhattan Gateway: New York's Pennsylvania Station.* Waukesha, Wis., 1996.

——.*When the Steam Railroads Electrified.* Milwaukee, Wis., 1974.

National Transportation Policy Study Commission. *National Transportation Policies through the Year 2000.* Washington, D.C., 1979.

Potter, Janet Greenstein. *Great American Railroad Stations.* New York, 1996.

Riddell, Doug. *From the Cab.* Pasadena, Calif., 1999.

Saunders, Richard. *The Railroad Mergers and the Coming of Conrail.* Westport, Conn., 1978.

Schafer, Mike. *All Aboard Amtrak.* Piscataway, N.J., 1991.

Solomon, Brian. *The American Diesel Locomotive.* Osceola, Wis., 1999.

——.*Railroad Stations.* New York, 1998.

Solomon, Brian and Mike Schafer. *New York Central Railroad.* Osceola, Wis., 1999.

Stilgoe, John R. *Metropolitan Corridor.* New Haven, Conn., 1983.

Talbot, F. A. *Railway Wonders of the World, Vols. 1 & 2.* London, 1914.

Thompson, Slason. *Short History of American Railways.* Chicago, 1925.

Thoms, William E. *Reprieve for the Iron Horse: The Amtrak Experiment—Its Predecessors and Prospects.* Baton Rouge, La., 1973.

Trewman, H. F. *Electrifcation of Railways.* London, 1920.

Westing, Frederic. *Penn Station: Its Tunnels and Side Rodders.* Seattle, Wash., 1977.

Wilner, Frank N. *The Amtrak Story*. Omaha, Neb., 1994.

Winchester, Clarence. *Railway Wonders of the World, Vols. 1 & 2*. London, 1935.

Zimmermann, Karl R. *Amtrak at Milepost 10*. Park Forest, Ill., 1981.

——. *The Remarkable GG1*. New York, 1977.

Periodicals

CTC Board—Railroads Illustrated, Ferndale, Wash.

Diesel Era, Halifax, Pa.

Jane's World Railways, London.

Locomotive & Railway Preservation, Waukesha, Wis. [no longer published]

Official Guide to the Railways, New York.

Passenger Train Annual, Nos. 3 & 4, Park Forest, Ill. [no longer published]

Passenger Train Journal, Waukesha, Wis. [no longer published]

RailNews, Waukesha, Wis. [no longer published]

Railroad History (formerly *Railway and Locomotive Historical Society Bulletin*), Boston, Mass.

Railway Age, Chicago and New York.

The Railway Gazette International, London.

TRAINS, Waukesha, Wis.

Today's Railways, Sheffield, U.K.

Vintage Rails, Waukesha, Wis. [no longer published]

Brochures, Catalogs, Manuals, Pamphlets, Rulebooks, and Timetables

Amtrak California. *California Car Operating Manual*, 1997.

Amtrak Operating Instructions F40PH/P30CH diesel-electric locomotives, 1983.

Amtrak Operation Instructions Superliner II, 1993.

Amtrak public timetables 1971 to 2004.

Conrail. *Pittsburgh Division, System Timetable No. 5*, 1997.

Electro-Motive Division. *SDP40F Operator's Manual, 2nd ed.* La Grange, Ill., 1974.

Eliot, Charles William. *Inscriptions over Pavilion Union Station Washington D.C.*, no date.

General Code of Operating Rules, 4th ed., 2000.

General Electric. *Dash 8 Locomotive Line*, no date.

——. *P32AC-DM Operating Manual*. Erie, Pa., 1995.

Metro-North Railroad. *Rules of the Operating Department*, 1999.

——. *Timetable No. 1.*, 2001.

NORAC Operating Rules, 7th ed., 2000.

Sikorsky Aircraft. *TurboTrain Operating Manual, Model TMT-3D*, no date.

INDEX